A Guide to
Supervision

A Guide to

Supervision

GEORGE R. TERRY

Late of Ball State University

LESLIE W. RUE

Georgia State University

LEARNING SYSTEMS COMPANY

A division of
RICHARD D. IRWIN, INC.   Homewood, Illinois   60430

The material published in this book is an adaptation of material previously published in a Programmed Learning Aid (PLAID) entitled *Supervision*.

ISBN 0-256-02570-3

Library of Congress Catalog Card No. 81-82997

Printed in the United States of America

1 2 3 4 5 6 7 8 9 0 K 9 8 7 6 5 4 3 2

INTRODUCTION

This Guide is a summary of the essential information needed for successful supervision. It provides a quick but comprehensive review of the basic fundamentals of supervision. Like other Irwin Publications for Professional Development, this book is ideal for self-study, reference, or review. It can also be used as a text for supervisory training.

A Guide to Supervision is written for use by experienced supervisors, relatively new supervisors, or people aspiring to become supervisors. It is equally applicable to supervisors in private enterprises or government, profit or not-for-profit organizations, and large or small organizations.

The basic essentials of supervision are presented in a logical and well-organized manner. Special efforts were made to present these essentials in a manner which would make them readily transferable to the "real world." Numerous practical examples are also offered.

The first author, the late George R. Terry, was well known and widely respected as a management educator and consultant. He was the author or co-author of numerous books including *Supervisory Management* and *Principles of Management,* both published by Richard D. Irwin, Inc. The second author, Leslie W. Rue, is also a successful educator, author, and consultant. Currently he is associate professor of management at Georgia State University, Atlanta. Dr. Rue is co-author of several other textbooks, including two with Richard D. Irwin, Inc.: *Management Theory and Application* and *Supervision: Key Link to Productivity.*

Topical outline of course content

Contents

Chapter 1

THE SUPERVISOR'S ROLE

Three basic types of management exist in most organizations. Top management of private enterprise organizations usually includes the chairman of the board, president, and senior vice presidents. This level of management establishes the goals of the organization and the policies necessary to achieve these goals. Middle management includes all employees below the top-management level who manage other managers. The supervisor's boss is normally a middle manager. Middle management develops departmental goals and policies necessary to achieve the organizational goals and policies. *The final level of management is the supervisor.* The supervisor manages operative employees. Operative employees are those employees who physically produce an organization's goods and services.

The makeup of supervisory jobs differs widely in scope and content. Many names are used to describe the people who supervise. These vary from industry to industry and include foreman, office manager, crew leader, and head nurse. Figure 1–1 summarizes some of the names given to these jobs in different organizations. Regardless of the name, the supervisor is the manager who serves as the link between the operative employees and all other managers.

There is no universally accepted definition of the term *supervision.* The following definition is used in this book: *Supervision is the process of encouraging the members of a work unit to contribute positively toward accomplishing the organization goals.* This means the supervisor does not do operative work but sees that it is accomplished through the efforts of others.

Because supervisors bridge the gap between management and the operating employees, they must try to satisfy the needs and expectations of both. This is no easy role to fill. Management expects supervisors to have technical knowledge of the work, to meet deadlines, and to operate the department within prescribed cost limitations. Supervisors are also expected to maintain the respect, cooperation, and loyalty of

FIGURE 1–1
Supervisory job titles

Training supervisor	Coordinator of budget and cost control
Employment supervisor	Training specialist
Records and materials supervisor	Coordinator of employee services
Welding foreman	Financial and accounting assistant
Steel foreman	Shift supervisor
Utility foreman	Records and documents supervisor
Powerhouse mechanic foreman	Training and safety supervisor
Assistant credit supervisor	Health physics supervisor
Administrative function supervisor	Receiving and warehousing supervisor
Meter routing supervisor	Farm supervisor
Residential supervisor	Leadman
Sensor graphics operator	Assistant cafeteria manager
Assistant supervisor of work processing	Supervisor for secretarial services
Office manager	

subordinates. Operative employees expect supervisors to be fair, to give honest appraisals of accomplishments, to help them develop the necessary skills and self-confidence, and to settle work differences.

WHERE DO SUPERVISORS COME FROM?

Most supervisors are promoted from the ranks of operative employees. Those with good technical skills and good work records are the employees normally selected by management for supervisory jobs. It is interesting to note that frequently union officers are chosen for supervisory jobs. Because union officers are elected, it is often assumed that

FIGURE 1–2
Progression of jobs into supervision

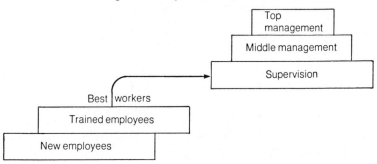

the voting employees view these people as having some leadership abilities. Thus, they are a natural source of talent for supervisory jobs. Another source is new college graduates. Many organizations today place new college graduates in supervisory jobs after a brief training period.

Figure 1–2 shows the normal progression into supervision. A person does not necessarily go into supervision and stop progressing. It is entirely possible to go from supervision all the way to the top of the organization. In fact, developing the proper skills required for supervision prepares a person for higher levels of management.

THE WORK OF A SUPERVISOR

The complex work of supervision is often categorized in four areas called the functions of supervision. These four functions are *planning, organizing, motivating,* and *controlling.* These functions make up the bulk of what a supervisor does. Planning involves determining the most effective means of achieving the work to be done. Organizing involves distributing the work among the work group and arranging the work so that it flows smoothly. The supervisor carries out the work of organizing through the general organizational structure that is established by higher levels of management. Thus, the supervisor functions within a general structure and is usually given specific work assignments from higher levels of management. The supervisor then sees that the specific work assignments are done. Motivating involves getting employees to put forth maximum effort while doing their jobs. Controlling provides for follow-up, with corrective action if needed to obtain satisfactory results.

Normally the supervisor spends more time on motivating and controlling than on planning and organizing. This happens because these functions are of greatest significance at the supervisory level. The supervisor's work is heavily oriented to helping operative employees achieve effective performance—a task intimately related to motivating and controlling.

The work of a supervisor can also be examined in terms of the types of skills required to do the work. Three basic skills can be isolated.

Technical skills: These refer to such things as job knowledge—knowledge of machines, processes, and methods of production.

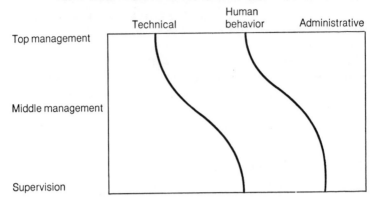

FIGURE 1–3
Mix of skills required for different management levels

Human relations skills: There refer to understanding human behavior and being able to work well with people.

Administrative skills: These refer to understanding the organization and how it works—understanding the planning, organizing, and controlling functions of supervision.

It is generally agreed that in most organizations, supervisors need a higher level of skill in the technical and human relations areas than in the areas of administration. The relative degree of skill changes as a person moves up in the managerial ranks. Figure 1–3 illustrates this concept. This does not imply that a supervisor needs more technical skills than a top manager, but rather that a supervisor needs more technical skills relative to the human behavior and administrative skills. A supervisor who has ambitions of moving up in the organization must also develop good administrative and human relations skills.

Comparing the supervisory level with other management levels reveals its unique characteristics and sheds additional light on the role of the supervisor. For example, consider who is supervised. Middle and top managers deal basically with other management members, who usually have similar objectives and talk a common language. Supervisors, however, devote most of their time to working with and achieving results through nonmanagement members, whose work philosophy, viewpoints, and language may differ significantly from their own. In addition, supervisors usually have more subordinates reporting directly to them than any member in the higher levels of management, and they tend to be limited to direct face-to-face management of group members.

A third difference is that supervisors' tasks are relatively more specialized and focus on particular functions. As a consequence, supervisors tend to visualize problems and opportunities in terms of their particular areas of concentration. But to climb the management hierarchy, they must eventually broaden their base and become competent in related specialized areas. Finally, there is a difference in the kinds of decisions made. Because they are in direct contact with operative employees, supervisors must interpret, apply, and make meaningful the directives and requirements laid down by their own managers. Usually these actions must be taken within a relatively short period of time.

THE SUPERVISOR'S AUTHORITY AND RESPONSIBILITY

To understand the role of a supervisor, the nature of his or her authority and responsibility must be considered. Authority can be viewed as the right to make decisions and to take action. This does not mean that supervisors have the right to order people around or to behave as dictators. Rather, they are to influence the actions of the people being supervised by directing, guiding, helping, correcting, and stimulating them.

Significant aspects of authority as applied by supervisors include the following:

1. Making decisions as needed and implementing them.
2. Recognizing that the authority exercised should take into account the probable reaction of the group and should consider the members' training, loyalty, beliefs, attitudes, and work behavior.
3. Considering facts along with judgments in all use of authority.
4. Encouraging employees to feel free to offer suggestions and ideas— to participate in the makeup of the authority used in any instance.
5. Keeping aware that employees are individuals whose degree of decision-making participation will vary with their interests, the possible effect of the decision upon them, and how they view the urgency of the situation.

Supervisory responsibility is being accountable for results. Being responsible is the same as being obligated. Ideally the boss and the supervisor mutually agree upon the desired result. The following are among the most helpful considerations concerning responsibility for the supervisor:

1. Knowing the objectives sought and making certain that employees know their individual objectives and how these contribute to the group's objectives.
2. Developing an effective team spirit.
3. Keeping all team members fully informed along with all other employees who interact with team members in the normal sequence of work events.
4. Dividing and assigning the work fairly and on a basis that is known and understood by all team members.
5. Interpreting policies, enforcing company regulations, and developing better work methods.

FACTORS LIMITING SUPERVISION

Under today's conditions there are several factors that limit a supervisor's actions. These factors must be recognized in order to understand the problems and the issues typically facing the supervisor. First, there is the question of how much influence and control of resources the supervisor can exercise. At one time the supervisor hired, fired, set the conditions of work, and was virtually unchallenged in what was decided. Today this is not true; many staff specialists are involved at the supervisory level. The formal authority of supervisors is now limited by such factors as the behavior and the beliefs of today's better educated and more informed employees, a host of governmental regulations, the practice of arbitration and appeal, and the access afforded by the open-door policy of middle and top managers.

A second factor that tends to limit the decision-making power of supervisors is the existence of unions. Although the supervisors are involved in discussions with the union regarding policy interpretation and grievances, the big issues are settled by higher-ups, and supervisors are expected to conform to these decisions.

A third limiting factor with which supervisors contend is the pressure under which they must operate. As mentioned earlier, today's supervisors do not have the time to reflect on all matters related to the work situation. There is constant pressure to get out the work, meet the budget, maintain quality, and compete for advancement with other supervisors.

WHY SUPERVISORS FAIL

Unfortunately supervisors fail for many reasons. By developing an understanding of these reasons, a supervisor can avoid many of them.

1. Inability or unwillingness to delegate work. This is a frequent cause of supervisory failure. Most supervisors are promoted from operative jobs and are accustomed to doing the physical work themselves. Supervisors are generally required to have technical skills in the jobs they are managing. Unfortunately, too many supervisors think that the technical skills alone are sufficient for success. However, human relations and administrative skills are also needed for success.

2. Improper use of authority. Some supervisors let their newfound authority go to their heads. It is sometimes difficult to remember that the use of authority alone does not get the support and cooperation of the employees. It is just as important to learn when not to use authority as to learn when to use it.

3. Trying to continue to be one of the gang. After being promoted into supervision, it is important to remember that a person is no longer one of the gang. Being a supervisor may require decisions that are not always popular. Thus, the supervisor must learn to maintain a balance between good human relations and being one of the gang. Because supervisors are the connecting link between other levels of management and the operative employees, they must learn to represent both groups.

4. Setting a poor example. A supervisor must always remember that the work group looks to the supervisor to set the example. Employees expect fair and equitable treatment from their supervisor. Unfortunately, too many supervisors play favorites and treat employees inconsistently. Government legislation has attempted to reduce this practice somewhat, but it is still a common problem.

5. A lack of desire for the job. Unfortunately, many people are promoted into supervision merely because of their technical skills, not because of their desire to be a supervisor. Regardless of one's technical skills, the desire to be a supervisor is necessary for success. Generally, this desire encourages a person to develop the other skills necessary in supervision—human relations skills and administrative skills.

These five reasons are certainly not the only ones that cause supervisory failure, but they represent some of the most common ones. Certainly the organization itself may be at fault if it does not provide for the proper selection and training of supervisory personnel.

Chapter 2

MAKING SOUND DECISIONS

One of the primary factors that distinguishes supervisors from operative employees is the level and types of decisions that must be made. Every working day supervisors are faced with many decision situations. The manner in which they react to these situations certainly has a major impact on supervisors' success.

TIMING THE DECISION

Recognizing the need to make a decision is a natural prerequisite to making a sound decision. Some supervisors always seem to make decisions on the spot, while others tend to take forever in deciding even a simple matter. Another familiar type is the person who just seems to ignore the entire matter by acting as if it doesn't exist. The supervisor who takes pride in making quick decisions is also running the risk of making bad decisions. Failure to gather and evaluate available data, to consider peoples' feelings, and to anticipate the impact of the decision can result in a very quick but poor decision. Of course the other extreme is just as risky—the supervisor who listens to the problem and promises to get back to the employee but never does. Nearly as bad is the supervisor who gets back to the employee but only after an inordinate amount of time. There are other familiar types: the supervisor who never seems to have adequate information to make a decision, the supervisor who frets and worries over even the simplest decisions, and the supervisor who refers everything to the boss.

In all of these profiles, the supervisor is concerned either too much or too little with making a decision. There is little regard to the timing and quality of the decision. Especially when the situation involves some unpleasantries (such as whether to fire an employee), it is common for the supervisor to make a quick decision and thus get rid of the problem. Another approach is to ignore the problem and hope that it will go away. These are *natural* human reactions. Successful supervisors learn to resist these reactions and to make decisions with a proper concern for timeliness.

Knowing when to make a decision is complicated by the fact that different decisions must be made within different time frames. For example, a supervisor would generally have much more time in deciding on committee appointments than what to do when three employees call in sick. Unfortunately, there is no magic formula to tell the supervisor when a decision should be made or how long it should take. The important thing is to develop an awareness for the importance of properly timing decisions.

Today's supervisor should also understand the relationship between proper timing of a decision and being decisive. Decisiveness is a very desirable and necessary characteristic of a good supervisor. To avoid or put off making a decision can result in worse circumstances than making a questionable but timely decision. However, being decisive does not necessarily mean making the decision in the least amount of time. Being decisive means making a decision in a reasonable amount of time.

IDENTIFY THE PROBLEM

Frequently the hardest part of making a decision is defining just what the decision problem is. It is very difficult for a supervisor to make a sound decision about anything unless the exact nature of the problem is known. For example, suppose a certain machine operator is producing an unacceptably high number of rejects. Is the problem due to the machine? The operator? The raw material? Or some other factor? Similarly, an employee complains about the work place being too hot. Is the temperature set too high? Is the employee just "hot natured?" Is something wrong with the air conditioner? Or is the employee just a complainer?

Many supervisors have a difficult time distinguishing between the symptoms of the problem and the problem itself. This often results in the supervisor treating the symptoms and not the problem. Treatment of the symptoms is usually a short-term solution at best. For

FIGURE 2–1
Factors to aid in defining the problem

Symptoms:	What has alerted you in the problem? How did you recognize the problem? What is wrong? Have there been any obvious changes?
Location:	Where are the symptoms occurring?
Time:	When did you discover the symptoms? How long have they existed?
Extent:	How severe does the problem appear to be?

example, suppose your car has a faulty generator that in turn causes the battery to run down. If you treat the symptom and replace the battery, you will have solved the problem only for a very short time.

Figure 2–1 presents four factors that when systematically addressed can help in defining the problem. The responses to each of these factors should be recorded in writing to help in being objective.

IDENTIFY POSSIBLE ALTERNATIVES

After the problem has been clearly defined, all possible alternatives can be identified. Obviously any decision is only as good as the best of the alternatives that are considered. One common pitfall in identifying possible alternatives is to consider only those which are obvious or those previously used. Such an approach can result in the exclusion of many viable alternatives. As a general rule, the more alternatives generated, the better the final solution. There is a great tendency among many supervisors to stop looking for alternatives once they have one or two that look acceptable. A good rule of thumb is to try to generate at least four alternatives.

Seeking the opinion of others who may know something about the problem can also be helpful. It is easy to become so involved in a particular problem that the supervisor cannot see the forest for the trees. In this type of situation, the supervisor becomes so engrossed in the details that alternatives, obvious to a person who is not as close to the problem, are overlooked.

GATHER FACTS

After identifying the problem and possible alternatives, the next step is to gather and organize facts that are relevant to the various

FIGURE 2–2
General questions to answer in the data gathering phase

Does company (organization) policy have anything to say about the decision at hand?

Has a similar situation occurred in the past? If so, what was done?

What are the costs involved?

How will this affect productivity? Work procedures? Employee morale?

alternatives. It is difficult, if not impossible, to make sound decisions without the pertinent facts. At the same time, however, it is rare that supervisors ever have *all* of the facts that they would like. Of course the timeliness of the decision has a major impact on how much data to gather and analyze. Successful supervisors learn to make decisions based on the available facts plus those which can be obtained within a reasonable amount of time and at a reasonable cost. Figure 2–2 lists some general questions that might be addressed in the fact gathering phase. It should also be mentioned that today's supervisor can be faced with the problem of too much information instead of not enough. Computers and modern technology have made information overload a real problem for many supervisors. This occurs when the supervisor receives irrelevant reports, computer printouts, and memos. It is not unusual for a simple and useful report to eventually evolve into a large, overburdened report with very little useful information. In this situation, the problem facing the supervisor is to sort out the relevant from the irrelevant information.

EVALUATE ALTERNATIVES

Once the general questions shown in Figure 2–2 have been analyzed and the appropriate data gathered, the next step is to evaluate each of the alternatives. Generally this involves a comparison of costs involved, time required to implement, and the expected end results. Using the collected data, the supervisor should project what would happen if each of the different alternatives was implemented. How long would it take to implement? How much would it cost? What would be the favorable and unfavorable outcomes? It is usually helpful to develop a system for recording the evaluations in some type of written form. Figure 2–3 contains an example format. One major advantage to such an approach is that all the alternatives can be compared

FIGURE 2–3
Example format for evaluating alternatives

	Alternative	Time required to implement	Estimated costs	Favorable points of outcome	Unfavorable points of outcome
A	Repair machine	15 days	$2,000	Workers are familiar with the machine; it has proven itself.	Might break down again soon; not as fast as new machine; take longer to fix.
B	Replace with reconditioned machine	8 days	$4,500	Same as old machine; no training necessary.	Reconditioned machine may not last as long as new one; not as fast as some new ones.
C	Replace with new but identical machine	5 days	$6,000	Same as old machine; no training necessary; likely to last a long time.	Relatively expensive.
D	Replace with new, modernized machine	5 days	$7,000	Fastest machine available; likely to last a long time.	Most expensive, operator will require some training.

at the same time. Another advantage is that all alternatives can be evaluated using the same categories of information. Such an approach provides much more objectivity than a simple mental evaluation of the alternatives.

CHOOSE AND IMPLEMENT THE BEST ALTERNATIVE

Choosing the best or most desirable alternative is not always as easy as it seems. Certainly this step is made easier if the previous steps in the decision-making process were thoroughly done. After the costs, time, and potential outcomes have been evaluated, the decision often still requires some judgment and even willpower on the part of the supervisor. While some alternatives can usually be eliminated immediately after the data have been collected, others require a closer look. In these situations, the supervisor draws upon experience, intuition, and suggestions from others in making the final choice. Caution is necessary in this state so that personal biases and prejudices do not influence the decision.

It is not unusual for a supervisor to select the best of the alternatives being considered even if none appears to be satisfactory. The tendency here is to select an alternative and thus make the decision. In essence, completing the decision becomes more important than the decision itself. In such situations, a viable alternative that should be considered and evaluated is to do nothing. This alternative gives the supervisor time to go back and seek some additional alternatives.

After the final decision has been made, the supervisor should take the necessary steps to implement the decision. This includes assigning responsibilities, communicating the timetable to be followed, outlining the types of control to be used, and identifying any potential problems. Experience has shown that employees and people in general are much less resistant to a decision when they understand the why, when, and who of the decision. When communicating the decision to the affected parties, the supervisor should explain why the decision was necessary, why the specific alternative was chosen, what actions are required, and what results are expected.

A final phase of the decision-making process is to evaluate the decision. Basic questions need to be answered. Did the decision achieve the desired results? If not, what went wrong? Why? The answers to these questions can be of great help when a similar situation presents itself in the future. The key here is to learn from the past and apply this knowledge to future decisions.

THE USE OF GROUP PARTICIPATION

You are familiar with the old saying that two heads are better than one. This is true in many decision situations. There are many advantages to involving the members of the work group in the decision. Most obvious is the fact that with several people participating there are naturally more resources to call upon. This usually results in the genera-

FIGURE 2–4
Positive and negative aspects of group decision making

Positive aspects of group decisions
1. The sum total of the group's knowledge is greater.
2. The group generally develops a much wider range of alternatives.
3. Participation increases the acceptability of the decision to the group.
4. Group members better understand why a decision was made.

Negative aspects of group decisions
1. Take more time.
2. One individual may dominate and/or control the group.
3. Pressures to conform may inhibit group members.
4. Competition can become overly intense among the group members.
5. Groups have a tendency to accept the first potentially positive alternative.

tion of more and better alternatives. A second and equally important advantage results in commitment to the decision by the members of the group. People more readily accept decisions they have participated in than those forced upon them. A person who participates in reaching a decision usually feels a commitment to make it work. The value of this approach is not limited to the final decision. A more complete understanding of what alternatives were considered and how each was evaluated can be of enormous help in getting the group to accept change. This is especially true if those who must implement the change are the ones who participated in the decision.

Group decisions can be very beneficial in certain situations. However, there are drawbacks that make individual decisions preferable in some situations. Because group decisions almost always require more time, an individual decision is generally best when there is a critical time limitation. Another potential problem with group decisions is the tendency of one person to dominate and control the group. The natural pressure to conform can also inhibit certain group members. Yet another possibility is for competition to develop within the group to such an extent that winning becomes more important than the issue itself. A final hazard is the tendency of groups to accept the first potentially positive solution and give little attention to other alternatives. In summary, group decisions are generally preferable where avoiding mistakes is of greater importance than speed. Figure 2–4 summarizes the positive and negative aspects of group decision making.

Brainstorming. Brainstorming is a form of group decision making that involves presenting a problem and then allowing the group to develop ideas for solutions. In order to encourage the free flow of ideas, no criticisms of suggested solutions are allowed initially. After and only after all ideas have been presented and recorded does the group begin to evaluate the ideas. The basic approach is to encourage all participants to throw out any and all ideas that come to mind. The ideas may be wide and seemingly impractical, but they may lead to a creative solution. In addition to the above rules, other suggestions have been found helpful in generating success in brainstorming. Ideally a session should last from 45 minutes to an hour. The problem to be considered should not be discussed before the session. A small-sized room and conference table should be used to encourage free-flowing communication.

Brainstorming is most applicable to simple decision problems requiring creative ideas. Naming a new product or service, coming up with a new use for a product, and identifying new ways to reduce wasted time are some examples of situations where brainstorming might be used. Unfortunately, brainstorming is not very useful in helping to make decisions dealing with risk or uncertainty—such as whether or not to hire a certain person.

TYPICAL TRAPS TO AVOID

Many supervisors have a tendency to fall into one or more traps when making decisions. Some of the most frequently encountered of these traps are discussed below.

Trap 1: Making all decisions BIG decisions. Everyone has run into the supervisor who treats every decision as if it were a life-or-death issue. This supervisor spends two hours deciding whether to order one or two boxes of rubber bands. Not only does this approach waste much of the supervisor's time, but it also keeps the employees confused—the employees have a hard time distinguishing between the important and not-so-important issues. This approach can also result in the really important problems not receiving proper attention because the supervisor becomes bogged down with unimportant problems. This type of supervisor must learn to allocate an appropriate amount of time to each decision based on its relative importance.

Trap 2: Creating crisis situations. Some supervisors seem to delight in turning all decision situations into crisis situations. A true crisis occurs when the decision must be made under extreme time constraints.

In actuality, very few crises occur naturally. What happens is that a normal situation is transferred into a crisis situation by the supervisor. Even when a true crisis does occur, the supervisor must learn to remain calm and think clearly. It is a good habit to always ask yourself, "How much time do I *really* have to make this decision?" It is easy and even natural to assume that you have less time than you actually do.

Trap 3: Failing to consult with others. The advantages of consulting others in the decision-making process were discussed earlier. However, some supervisors are reluctant to seek outside opinions.

They fear that asking advice will make them look inadequate. Many supervisors, especially new ones, are under the impression that they should know all the answers and are hesitant to ask someone else's opinion. These are *natural* tendencies and should be recognized as such. Successful supervisors learn to put good sense and reasoning ability ahead of ego.

Trap 4: Never admitting a mistake. No one makes the best decision every time. If a supervisor makes a bad decision, it is best to admit it and do what is necessary to correct it. The worst possible course is to try to force a bad decision into being a good decision. For example, suppose you go out and buy a used car. After you have owned the car for a couple of months, it becomes apparent that the car is a lemon. It would probably be much better to admit the mistake and get rid of the car, even at a loss, than to pretend that it was a good decision and continue to pour more money into the car. Again, it is a natural tendency not to want to admit mistakes.

Trap 5: Constantly regretting decisions. The opposite effect from Trap 4 can also occur. Some supervisors seem to forever regret their decisions—the good ones as well as the bad ones. These people always want to change the unchangeable. A typical sentence starts with, "I sure wish I had. . . ." Once a decision has been made and is final, don't brood over it. Remember very few decisions are totally bad. Some are just better than others. Too often a supervisor will spend time dreaming about "what ifs" and not enough time implementing the current decision.

Trap 6: Failing to utilize precedents and policies. Why reinvent the wheel? If a similar decision situation has occurred in the past, supervisors should draw upon that previous experience. If a certain situation seems to be constantly recurring, it is usually helpful to implement a policy covering the situation. For example, it is wise to have

FIGURE 2–5

Positive points	Rating	Negative points	Rating
David is a quick learner.	5	David is frequently late.	6
David gets along with other employees	2	David has been absent six days.	7
David has proven he can do the job	9	David's personal appearance could be better.	4
David presently has six months of training experience, and it would be costly to hire another person.	8	David has only two years of college.	2
After David arrives at work he has a good attitude.	6		—
Score	30	Score	19

Positive Score	30
Negative Score	−19
Total Score	11

a policy covering priorities for vacation time. Also, supervisors should develop an awareness of current organizational policies. These can often help in decision situations.

Suppose you are a supervisor for the First Trust Bank and David Dews is one of your tellers. Ever since David started to work for the bank almost six months ago, you have had problems with his attendance and promptness. On the other hand, David has learned quickly and his general job performance has been good. The end of David's probationary period is nearing, and you must make a recommendation concerning his future at the bank. You developed the positive and negative lists shown in Figure 2-5 and then rated each factor.

The positive factors greatly outweigh the negatives in David's case. The primary benefit of using this system is to identify the pertinent facts so that an objective evaluation can be made. This approach is simple and it requires very little time.

Chapter 3

OBJECTIVES AND SUPERVISION

The primary purpose of a supervisor is to see that the work is completed satisfactorily and on schedule. A supervisor must work effectively with subordinates, management members, and those outside the organization. Technical know-how is also necessary. The most important aspect of supervision, however, is objective achievement. The objectives that have been set for the group must be met. All work activities should be related to these stated objectives. Success in supervision depends on the supervisor's ability to identify objectives and to point all group efforts toward their achievement.

OBJECTIVES

Objectives (or goals) are concerned with direction and destination; they outline the desired results. The terms *goals* and *objectives* are used interchangeably throughout this text.

Objectives enable supervisors to focus directly on targets to be achieved within a given period. Supervisors' success depends upon their understanding of these objectives. Similarly, supervisors must be able to communicate these objectives to the employees who will actually perform the tasks necessary to achieve them.

At the supervisory level, objectives typically deal with quantity, quality, cost, and production levels. How these objectives are determined and how they are stated can have a great deal to do with how successful a supervisor might be in reaching them. Objectives should be looked upon as viable statements that add direction to all efforts.

USING OBJECTIVES IN SUPERVISION

Objectives can be utilized to develop the job skills of employees. When employees demonstrate a capacity for further growth, their objectives should be adjusted so that they can seek further achievements. The setting of new goals points the way and serves as a stimulus for greater performance. The more conventional method of turning talented employees loose to see what they can do on their own does not provide a target toward which to aim efforts and evaluate progress. It is better to adjust the objectives for such employees so that they will acquire new learning and additional talents. In such cases, the supervisor should share information, give counsel, and make certain the new goals call for excellence in performance. It is helpful to relate the work goals to the employees' personal goals whenever possible. Exceptionally capable employees are usually eager to discuss their careers with supervisors. Such discussions are mutually helpful because they reveal whether the right course is being pursued in view of the goals of both employees and supervisors.

Objectives can also provide help for the marginal employee. The supervisor might find out whether such an employee understands the work goals, what is expected, and what constitutes satisfactory performance. Does the employee lack required skill and knowledge? Does the employee's work attitude need reshaping? Is more feedback about the work needed?

ESTABLISHING OBJECTIVES

Supervisory objectives are usually derived from the plans and objectives of higher levels of management. They set the work targets that the department or work group is expected to achieve. Normally, supervisory objectives are expressed in detail, are precise, and are of a short-range nature. In fact, the majority of supervisory objectives deal with weekly, monthly, or quarterly time periods.

Objectives should span all significant areas of the department. This usually means that several objectives must be set. The problem with a single objective is that it is often achieved at the expense of other desirable objectives. For example, a supervisor may go all out to achieve a production objective, even if it means lowering quality. Objectives that have the best chance for success should have the following characteristics:

1. Objectives should be measurable or verifiable. Generally, the objectives should be expressed in quantitative terms and should include a stated time frame for completion. Avoid the use of words such as

FIGURE 3–1
Examples of how to improve work objectives

Poor:	To maximize production.
Better:	To increase production by 10 percent within the next three months.
Poor:	To reduce absenteeism.
Better:	To average no more than three absent days per employee per year.
Poor:	To waste less raw material.
Better:	To waste no more than 2 percent of raw material.
Poor:	To improve the quality of production.
Better:	To produce no more than two rejects per hundred units of production.

maximize, minimize, and *reduce.* An objective to "minimize costs" is commendable but not measurable. How does a supervisor ever know if costs have been minimized? In reality, the only way to truly minimize costs is to have zero costs! A much better way of stating this objective would be "to reduce costs by 5 percent by the end of next quarter."

2. The objective setting process should involve those responsible for achieving the objective. Most employees want to participate and be asked for their opinions and suggestions. Employees are more committed to the successful achievement of objectives that they have helped develop. Objectives that are simply announced by the supervisor are less likely to be achieved. Another good reason for involving the employees is that they frequently have valuable information to contribute. Being near to, and actually performing, the work provides insight and practical experience that the supervisor might not have.

3. The objectives should be challenging but realistic. Some people think that objectives should be set just slightly higher than can be attained. The thought here is to keep the employee stretching and to avoid a possible letdown that might occur once the objective is reached. One problem with this approach is that it only takes a short time for employees to figure out that the objective is unattainable. This can quickly demotivate employees. People are motivated by achieving difficult, but not impossible, goals. Another fallacy of this approach is that most people are turned on, not off, upon reaching a challenging goal. The key is for the objective to be challenging and realistic. Employees should be required to "reach," but the objective should also be within their capabilities.

4. Objectives should be regularly updated. All too often objectives are never updated. Pursuing outdated objectives wastes resources.

FIGURE 3–2
Typical areas of supervisory objectives

1. Production or Output: Usually expressed as number of units per time period.

   Example: Our objective is to average 20 widgets per hour.

2. Quality: Usually expressed as number of rejects, number of customer complaints, amount of scrap.

   Example: Our objective is to produce fewer than 10 rejects per week.

3. Personnel: Usually expressed in terms of turnover, absenteeism, tardiness.

   Example: Our objective is to average less than three days absenteeism per employee per year.

4. Training: Usually expressed in terms of hours of training exposure, number of classes attended, or knowledge gained.

   Example: Our objective is for every employee of the department to attend at least one full day at a training workshop within the next 12 months.

Objectives should be reviewed periodically. Those no longer of value should be discarded. Others will need revising in light of recent changes.

5. Objectives should be assigned priorities. Having several objectives does not mean that they are all of equal importance. The supervisor, as well as the employees, should know the relative importance of the objectives. This allows everyone to budget their time accordingly. In the event that problems occur, everyone should know what is most and least important.

Figure 3–1 presents some examples of how some poorly stated objectives might be better stated. Figure 3–2 shows some typical areas in which a supervisor might set objectives.

PERSONAL OBJECTIVES

In addition to work objectives, everyone has personal objectives. It is natural for most people to want to achieve certain things. Personal objectives deal with these wants. Because these objectives personalize and reinforce the work objectives, their accomplishment is necessary to get maximum individual performance.

General statements that characterize individuals' attitudes toward personal goals include the following:

1. All people have highly personalized goals. Personal goals greatly influence people's behavior; they are foremost in their thoughts and embody the peak of their ambitions. Finding out what these goals are, understanding them, and helping individuals satisfy them in their work efforts is one of the keys to successful supervision.

2. All people want to feel they are doing something worthwhile. Ideally, this worthwhile endeavor is undertaken for someone held in high esteem. Here the challenge to the supervisor is to strive to be a person for whom worthwhile endeavors will be made. That way, personal goals can work for the supervisor, and at the same time the employee gains needed satisfaction from work.

3. All people want to progress. People must feel they are making progress toward personal objectives in order to be satisfied. Goals inspire a desire to achieve; in fact, merely having a goal will normally be accompanied by thoughts of how to accomplish it.

4. All people condition their beliefs and thoughts by comparing themselves with others. People do not live alone; they are a part of society. They constantly compare themselves with others in order to estimate their own accomplishments.

MANAGEMENT BY OBJECTIVES (MBO)

Management by objectives (MBO) is a style of supervising based on a cooperative approach to setting objectives. Under management by objectives, all employees have a part in determining work objectives and the means for achieving these objectives. Supervisors and employees jointly agree on what the employees' work objectives will be and how they should be pursued. The key to success here is that supervisors and employees have an open exchange of ideas. After the work objectives and the means for achieving these objectives have been agreed upon, employees have a blueprint of the work results they are expected to achieve.

In management by objectives, the emphasis is not on the performance of job activities but on the accomplishment of results. Self-directives, highly personalized supervision, and encouragement to the individual to operate as a whole person within the context of the organization are features of MBO. Supervisors serve as resource people to assist all employees to reach their agreed-upon objectives. In effect,

FIGURE 3–3
Guidelines for setting individual objectives

1. Adapt your objectives directly to organizational goals and strategic plans. Do not *assume* that they support higher level management objectives.
2. Quantify and target the results whenever possible. Do not formulate objectives whose attainment cannot be measured or at least verified.
3. Test your objectives for challenge and achievability. Do not build in cushions to hedge against accountability for results.
4. Adjust the objectives to the availability of resources and the realities of organizational life. Do not keep your head either in the clouds or in the sand.
5. Establish reliable performance reports and milestones that measure progress toward the objective. Do not rely on instinct or crude benchmarks to appraise performance.
6. Put your objectives in writing and express them in clear, concise, and unambiguous statements. Do not allow them to remain in loose or vague terms.
7. Limit the number of statements of objectives to the *most* relevant key-result areas of your job. Do not obscure priorities by stating too many objectives.
8. Communicate your objectives to your subordinates so that they can formulate their own job objectives. Do not demand that they do your goal setting for you.
9. Review your statements with others to assure consistency and mutual support. Do not fall into the trap of setting your objectives in a vacuum.
10. Modify your statements to meet changing conditions and priorities.
11. Do not continue to pursue objectives that have become obsolete.

Source: From *Managing by Objectives* by Anthony P. Raia. Copyright 1974 by Scott Foresman and Company. Reprinted by permission of the publisher.

all employees become supervisors of their own work and are free to act within the outlined constraints.

Periodic progress reviews are essential to MBO. During a progress review, all employees are given direct feedback on actual performance as compared to planned performance (objectives). The manner in which feedback is given is important. If supervisors give the feedback in a downgrading or hostile fashion, then performance may be reduced. It is important to let employees know how they are doing and to identify areas where supervisors might provide help. Supervisors act as counselors and problem solvers *with* employees, not *to* employees. Usually, it is recommended that this feedback be provided formally two or three times each year.

A final requirement of MBO is that the employees be rewarded on the basis of objective attainment. This means that employee rewards are directly linked to the results attained as measured by the agreed-upon objectives. MBO can only work when the employees believe that rewards are dependent upon results.

One of the most difficult parts of an MBO system is deciding in what areas to set objectives. A helpful approach is for the individual to answer the following questions: How would I most like to be evaluated on my job? What things or areas should my boss look at to evaluate my performance? The answers to these questions provide the areas for setting objectives. If an individual has difficulty answering the above questions, then there is a good chance that the individual does not thoroughly understand his or her job. Figure 3–3 provides some additional tips for setting individual objectives.

MBO is not a panacea. Management by objectives is not a panacea for all supervisory ills. Like all supervisory styles, it must be applied with care. Of prime importance is the question of whether the employee understands, wants, and is capable of operating under the management by objectives approach. The employee must desire self-commitment, self-improvement, and self-control. Similarly, the supervisor must be willing to provide the necessary assistance, encouragement, and flexibility.

MBO is most effective when it is used at all levels of the organization. Under this situation, the objectives at each level should contribute to achieving the objectives at the next higher level. However, MBO can be implemented in the supervisor's department even if it doesn't exist at other levels. In either case, MBO will not succeed on its virtues alone. It must have the full attention of the supervisor and the employees, it must be thoroughly understood by everyone involved, and it must be given adequate time to succeed. To expect favorable results within a specified time period such as 30 to 60 days is unrealistic. In fact, it is not unusual at all for an MBO system to require up to a year for successful implementation. Such a time frame provides adequate time for educating both the supervisor and the employees on MBO.

Chapter 4

SUPERVISORY PLANNING AND CONTROL

Two of the most important functions performed by the supervisor are planning and controlling. Planning deals with commitments to future actions, and controlling deals with checking up and seeing to it that the results of the planned actions are met.

The supervisor must plan the department's work if it is to be done effectively, properly, and on time. Failure of the supervisor to plan can result in lost time, wasted materials, and misued equipment and space. After planning has been completed and the resulting plan has been developed and implemented, the supervisor must then control the plan. This involves seeing that the plan is carried out. Thus, planning and controlling are very closely related activities of supervision.

PLANNING

Planning is not concerned with future decisions, but rather with the future impact of today's decisions. When planning, supervisors should think about how today's decisions might affect future actions. Planning involves deciding what actions to take in order to accomplish known objectives. Some think of planning as including the objective setting process. In this case, planning is viewed in the broader sense of deciding what objectives to pursue and what to do in order to achieve those objectives. Whether or not the objective setting process is viewed as a part of the planning process or as a precedent of it, objectives must be established before the planning process can be completed. Obviously, it is not possible for supervisors to outline a course of action for reaching an objective if they do not know what the objective is. Since objectives were covered extensively in the previous chapter, this chapter will focus on the action part of the overall planning process.

THE SUPERVISOR'S ROLE IN PLANNING

In many cases, the supervisor receives planning information from higher levels in the organization. Frequently the supervisor is also consulted and participates in higher level planning activities, especially on matters dealing with personnel and equipment. The exchange of ideas and information between higher management and supervisors not only makes for better and more practical plans, it also keeps supervisors fully informed and updated as to what is going on.

It is common practice for upper management to plan down to the department level, but not within it. The supervisor is expected to make the detailed plans for the department. Furthermore, the supervisor is expected to handle departmental planning adjustments that arise due to changes and emergencies within the department. Upper level planning is usually relatively long range covering perhaps six months, a year, or two years. In contrast, the supervisor's planning is typically short range—of the near-at-hand, day-to-day, week-to-week variety.

DEVELOPING A PLAN

In developing a plan, it is useful to ask certain questions. By addressing each of these questions, the supervisor can work out the details of exactly how to proceed. This process can also help to identify potential problems.

1. What must be done? Precisely, what actions must be taken to reach the stated objectives? The supervisor must be sure that all actions taken contribute to the accomplishment of the objectives.

2. Why must it be done? This question serves as a check on question 1. Are the actions really necessary? Can the use of resources be justified?

3. When should it be done? The supervisor must decide how to coordinate the necessary actions with other activities. Dates and times should be selected and coordinated.

4. Who should do it? The supervisor must decide what skills and abilities are required. Once this has been established, the appropriate personnel must be identified.

5. Where should it be done? This question is closely related to question four. Where will the necessary people and equipment be located?

**FIGURE 4–1
The planning process**

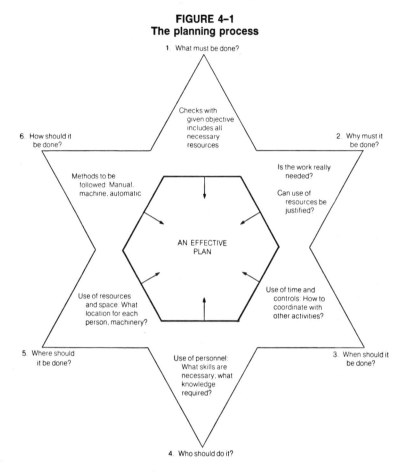

1. What must be done?

6. How should it
   be done?

Checks with
given objective
includes all
necessary
resources

2. Why must it
   be done?

Is the work really
needed?

Can use of
resources be
justified?

Methods to be
followed: Manual,
machine, automatic

AN EFFECTIVE
PLAN

Use of resources
and space: What
location for each
person, machinery?

Use of time and
controls: How to
coordinate with
other activities?

5. Where should
   it be done?

Use of personnel:
What skills are
necessary; what
knowledge
required?

3. When should it
   be done?

4. Who should do it?

6. How should it be done? What methods and procedures will be used? Can existing procedures be used or must new ones be developed? The planning process is summarized in Figure 4–1.

RESOURCE ALLOCATION

The previous sections discussed the overall framework for supervisory planning. Within this framework, supervisors regularly engage in certain specific planning activities. Resource allocation and scheduling are two of the most common planning-related activites performed by supervisors.

Resource allocation refers to the efficient allocation of people, materials, and equipment in order to successfully meet the objectives that have been established. Resource allocation determines what work will be performed by what person and/or machine and under what conditions. The materials needed must be determined and ordered. The work must be distributed to the different work stations. Personnel requirements must be determined and time requirements established for each stage of the process. In order to be able to efficiently allocate resources, supervisors often find it helpful to study the product or service route through the facility.

Routing. Routing involves determining the best sequence of operations. Routing attempts to make optimum use of the existing equipment and personnel through careful assignment of resources. At the same time, however, the desired level of output and the available mix of equipment and personnel place constraints on the sequence of operations. Although a route may appear to be fixed because of certain physical limitations, it should always be carefully analyzed.

Flowcharting and other graphical diagrams are used to aid in detecting and eliminating inefficiencies in a route. Flowcharts analyze a certain sequence of operations in a step-by-step fashion. Assembly charts and flow process charts are two common types of flowcharts. Assembly charts define the sequence and manner in which the various components of a product or service are assembled. Assembly charts typically provide an overall view of how the various parts fit together. A flow process chart outlines what happens to the product or service as it progresses through the department. Most flow process charts are much more detailed than assembly charts.

SCHEDULING

Scheduling develops the precise timetable that is to be followed in producing the products or services. Scheduling, per se, does not involve determining how long a job will take, but rather involves determining when the work will be performed. If schedulers do not already have a good feel for how long the different jobs will take, they must get this information before the schedule can be completed. The purpose of scheduling is to help assure that the work is synchronized and completed within certain time limits. Scheduling is naturally much easier if a thorough job has been done in analyzing the product or service route.

Determining and implementing priorities is a major part of scheduling. The supervisor must determine which items have high priorities and which have low priorities. This information may be given to the supervisor, or the supervisor may be required to make these decisions.

Anticipating lost time is also a requirement of scheduling. There is a great tendency on the part of many supervisors to try to schedule every minute of every working day. Such overscheduling can cause problems if a machine breaks down or if an employee is absent. At the same time, underscheduling can lead to idle equipment and personnel. Successful supervisors must learn to anticipate and schedule the unexpected.

Numerous types of scheduling tools have been developed to help visualize and simplify the scheduling problem. Most of these are adaptations of the Gantt chart. The different activities that are to be performed are usually listed vertically on a Gantt chart. Time is shown horizontally. By plotting the different activities and their respective times on a Gantt chart, the scheduler can visually determine when to schedule each activity. Figure 4–2 shows a Gantt chart for scheduling customer orders.

SUPERVISORY CONTROL

Controls should be desired to alert the supervisor to problems or potential problems before they become critical. Control means knowing

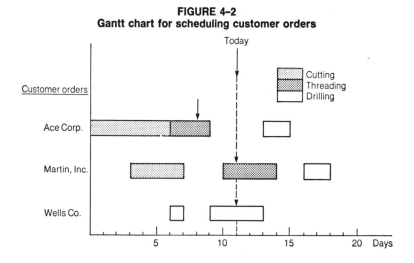

FIGURE 4–2
Gantt chart for scheduling customer orders

what is actually happening in comparison to what was planned. Controlling has many similarities to planning. The major difference between the two is that controlling usually takes place after the planning has been completed and implemented. Comparatively speaking, controlling is after the fact, whereas planning is before the fact. Control is accomplished by comparing actual performance to predetermined standards or objectives and then taking action to correct any deviations from the standard. Thus, the control process includes three primary steps: (1) establishing performance standards, (2) monitoring performance and comparing to standards, and (3) taking necessary corrective actions.

Establishing performance standards. A standard outlines what is expected. Standards are used to set performance levels for machines, tasks, individuals, groups of individuals, or even the organization as a whole. Usually standards are expressed in terms of quantity, quality, or time limitations. For example, standards may deal with production output per day, quality as reflected by customer service, or production schedules. Departmental and individual objectives can be used as standards for controlling departmental and individual performance.

The main purpose of performance standards is to answer the questions, "What is a fair day's work?" or "How good is good enough?" Although designed to reflect normal output, standards include more than just work. Output standards include allowances for rest, delays that occur as part of the job, time for personnel needs, time for equipment maintenance, and allowances for physical fatigue.

When possible, the management by objectives (MBO) approach should be used to set performance standards. In environments where MBO is not appropriate (such as with employees working on an assembly line), other approaches are available. One common approach is to use the judgment of the supervisor or other recognized experts. The problem with the approach is that it is very subjective in nature. The analysis of historical data such as production data is another approach. One potential problem here is that things may have changed since the data were collected. The most objective approach is based on industrial engineering methods. These methods usually involve a detailed and scientific analysis of the situation. Motion studies and time studies are examples of this approach.

Monitoring performance. The overriding purpose of monitoring performance is to provide information on what is actually happening. The major problems of monitoring performance are deciding when, where, and how often to monitor. The monitoring must be done often enough to provide adequate information. However, if overdone, it can become expensive and can also result in adverse reactions from employees. The key is to always view monitoring, not as a means of checking up on employees, but rather as a means of providing needed information. Thus, monitoring is preventative and not punitive in nature. In this same light, the reasons for monitoring should always be fully explained to the employees.

Timing is also important when monitoring performance. The supervisor must recognize a deviation in time to correct it. For example, raw materials must be ordered before they run out in order to allow for delivery time.

Most control tools and techniques are primarily concerned with monitoring performance. Reports, audits, budgets, and personal observations are all commonly used methods for monitoring performance. The Gantt chart that was discussed earlier as a scheduling tool can also be used as a monitoring device. This is done by graphically showing the work accomplished in relation to the work planned.

Taking corrective action. Only after the actual performance has been determined and compared to the standard can proper corrective action be determined. All too often, however, managers set standards and monitor performance but do not follow up with appropriate actions. If standards are not being satisfactorily met, the supervisor must find the cause of the deviation and correct it. A major problem in this step is determining when standards are not being satisfactorily met. How many mistakes should be allowed? Are the standards correctly set? Is the poor performance due to the employee or some other factor? These are the types of questions that the supervisor must answer before deciding on the appropriate corrective action.

Once a path of corrective action has been decided upon, it must be carefully implemented. The style and method used to take corrective action can greatly affect the results achieved. When the corrective action involves a supervisor's employees, the supervisor should fully explain why the action is necessary. All too often supervisors take corrective action without giving an adequate explanation. It is only natural behavior for employees to resist something that they know nothing about. Supervisors should also avoid talking down to subordinates when making corrections. People do not like to be talked to as if they are inferior.

THE POSITIVE APPROACH

Controlling should be looked upon as a positive, helpful activity that aids in the achievement of goals within the constraints of specified quantities, qualities, time use, and cost. It is more than a passive checkup. Properly implemented, good control efforts can be encouraging and helpful to employees. Supervisors should make it known that controls are designed to help employees win respect and recognition. It is rewarding for them to know and to be told officially that the group's accomplishments are satisfactory. It is also important for them to know what work performance is expected. If controlling is helpful, meaningful, and acceptable to employees, they can use it advantageously to attain effective self-direction.

Proper use of controlling also helps supervisors perform their work better. If they follow their plans and use adequate controls, their programs should have good results.

Chapter 5

ORGANIZING AND DELEGATING

Organizing is the grouping of activities necessary to reach common objectives. Organizing also involves the assignment of each grouping to a manager with the authority necessary to supervise the people performing the activities. Thus, the questions of who does what work and who tells who what work to do are addressed.

THE ORGANIZATION STRUCTURE

The organization structure results from the grouping of work activities and the assignment of each grouping to a manager. Generally, the organization structure is developed by upper levels of management. However, it is important that supervisors know and understand the makeup of the total organization. They must be familiar with what the total organization is meant to do and with the role that each part plays in accomplishing the total job. This knowledge helps supervisors to understand their jobs, to work with other supervisors, and to know what to delegate.

THE SUPERVISOR AND AUTHORITY

Authority is the right to command and expend resources. The lines of authority are established by the organization structure and link the various organizational units together. Supervisors' authority is determined by upper levels of management and is implemented through the organization structure. The amount of authority given to supervisors varies with the situation. For example, some supervisors may be given much more authority to make work assignments than others. It is not unusual for supervisors to have the authority to organize the work unit within broad and general guidelines. Additionally, supervisors must usually structure their own jobs.

FIGURE 5–1
Typical supervisory responsibilities

1. Assign specific duties to each subordinate.
2. Determine the amount of work to be accomplished by each subordinate.
3. Transfer members within your department.
4. Authorize overtime.
5. Answer questions about time standards.
6. Make suggestions for improvements in work procedures.
7. Work with appropriate staff groups to develop and implement better work methods.
8. Counsel employees.
9. Process grievances with shop stewards.
10. Participate in drawing up departmental budgets.
11. Authorize repair and maintenance work.
12. Maintain production records.

One thing that can make the organizational aspects of a supervisor's job difficult is the special projects or emergency work that often occur. These special projects are usually in addition to the normal, day-to-day work. Special projects are activities that have an identifiable beginning and end and are nonroutine in nature. The priorities associated with different projects will naturally vary. The amount of notice that the supervisor receives concerning the project also varies with the project. Emergencies are usually totally unpredictable and generally carry a high priority. While it is not possible to eliminate all emergencies, good organization and good planning can reduce their occurrence.

THE SUPERVISOR AND RESPONSIBILITY

Responsibility is accountability for reaching objectives, using resources properly, and adhering to organizational policy. Once supervisors accept responsibility, they become obligated to perform the assigned work. The term *responsibility* as defined above should not be confused with the term *responsibilities* as used in defining job duties. When used in defining job duties, responsibilities refer to the things that make up supervisors' jobs. Figure 5–1 lists some typical supervisory responsibilities.

LINE VERSUS STAFF

Within the organization structure, there are two major types of authority: (1) line and (2) staff. Line authority is the superior-subordinate relationship and forms a direct line from the top to the bottom of the organizational structure. Line managers and line employees are directly involved in producing and marketing the organizations' goods or services. For example, assembly-line supervisors are line employees in that they are directly involved in producing the organization's goods. Bank tellers are also line employees because they are directly involved in providing the organization's services.

Staff authority is entirely different. Staff authority is used to support and advise line authority. It is helpful to think of staff as being "nonline" and as being designed to contribute to the efficiency and maintenance of the organization. Staff personnel are generally specialists in a particular field. For example, the personnel department is normally considered to have staff authority. This authority is normally limited to making recommendations to the line personnel. Customarily the staff manager exercises authority *to* a line of authority, whereas the line manager exercises authority *along* a line of authority.

Most organizations today are line and staff—meaning that the structure has both management members with line authority and management members with staff authority. The largest number of supervisors are line employees.

INFORMAL ORGANIZATION

There is a natural tendency for people having common work, goals, or social interests to band together in groups. These groups make up the informal organizations that exist whenever groups of people are brought together. The informal organization exists within, and in addition to, the formal organization. Men and women like working with people they know and who in turn know them. People who do the same type of work or have common interests are likely to form informal groups. Frequent face-to-face meetings, discussions, and dedication to a common cause help informal groups to evolve, grow, and prosper.

Since the informal organization has an indefinite, ever-changing structure (members come and go, purposes change, interests are altered), it is vulnerable to manipulation and opportunism. It may be very difficult to define the informal organization in a particular company, but it does exist. It cannot be destroyed because it is a natural outcome of people working together. Therefore the supervisor should acknowledge the presence of the informal organization and work with it in ways that will aid supervision. For example, the informal organization can be used to disseminate information and to gain acceptance of new ideas. The supervisor should know the informal leaders, enlist their help, listen to their suggestions, and consult with them in reaching major decisions. The informal organization is discussed at length in Chapter 9.

DELEGATING AUTHORITY AND RESPONSIBILITY

Failure to delegate is probably the most frequent reason that supervisors fail. Delegation is an art. Unfortunately, it does not come naturally for many people. In its most common use, delegation refers to the delegation of authority. To delegate authority means to grant or confer authority from one person to another. Generally authority is delegated in order to assist receiving parties in completing their assigned duties. For example, a supervisor may give employees the authority to organize their own work, as long as they meet the production requirements.

There is considerable debate about the delegation of responsibility. Some people say you can delegate responsibility, while others say you can't. A close analysis of the issue generally reveals that the debate is more a communication problem than a misunderstanding of the concepts involved. Those saying that responsibility cannot be delegated support their position by stating that supervisors can never shed the responsibilities of their jobs by passing them onto their employees. Those saying that responsibility can be delegated justify their position by pointing out that supervisors can certainly make their employees responsible for certain actions. Both parties are correct. Supervisors can delegate responsibilities in the sense of making their employees responsible for certain actions. However, this delegation does not make supervisors any less responsible. Thus, delegation of responsibility does not mean abdication of responsibility by the delegating party. Responsibility is *not* like an object that can be passed from individual to individual.

Successful delegation involves three basic steps: (1) assigning work to the different members of the work group, (2) creating an obligation (responsibility) on the part of each employee to the delegating supervisor to perform the duties satisfactorily, and (3) granting permission (authority) to take the actions necessary to perform the duties. Thus, successful delegation involves the delegation of both authority and responsibility.

WHY SUPERVISORS ARE RELUCTANT TO DELEGATE

The majority of supervisors are promoted into their supervisory positions from the ranks of the operative workers. Moving from operative worker to supervisor presents some differences that can affect a new supervisor's ability to delegate. As an operative worker, a person's performance is, for the most part, entirely a function of what he or she does. In other words, operative employee's performance is not normally dependent on anyone else. As supervisors, however, these same people's performance is almost totally dependent on the performance of others—namely the employees directly responsible to them. The problem occurs when supervisors do not fully realize this difference, and rather than concentrate on the functions of supervision, spend the majority of their time trying to do everyone else's job. The justification running through the supervisors' minds is that the way for them to look good is to ensure that everyone's job is done right. This is a very natural trap to fall into. It also provides the foundation for most of the reasons why supervisors are reluctant to delegate.

If you want anything done right, do it yourself. Many supervisors subscribe to the old saying, "If you want anything done right, do it yourself!" This attitude reveals that supervisors not only do not understand the supervisory process, but also shows that supervisors have done a poor job of selecting and training their employees. Supervisors who attempt to do it all themselves or to prove that they are superior operative workers find that their time is consumed by rather unimportant tasks. Thus, they do not have time to perform their supervisory tasks.

It is easier to do it myself. Supervisors often say that it is easier for them to do the job than to explain it to their employees. While this may be true in some cases, it usually represents a very short-sighted view. It may be easier for the supervisor to do the task the 1st time or even the 5th time, but is it still easier the 20th or 50th time? In other words, it may require some investment of the supervisor's time to train the employees to do the job, but this is usually the best approach.

Fear of an employee looking too good. The fear that an employee will "look so good that the employee might replace the supervisor" can inhibit some supervisors from delegating. Such fears are totally unfounded for good supervisors. A supervisor's performance is, for the most part, a reflection of the performance of his or her employees. If supervisors' employees look good, the supervisor looks good. If the employees look bad, the supervisor looks bad.

More confidence in doing the detail work. Some supervisors feel much more confident when doing the detail and operative work than when performing their supervisory functions. Most people have some fear of the unknown and tend to shy away from it. Thus, it is understandable that new supervisors would feel much more confident doing those things that they have had success with in the past.

Preconceived ideas about employees. Sometimes supervisors erroneously jump to conclusions concerning the capabilities of subordinates. For example, a supervisor might form a negative opinion about an employee's ability based on one occurrence. Further, this occurrence may be very unrepresentative of the employee, or the supervisor may be unaware of the circumstances surrounding the occurrence.

Desire to set the right example. Most supervisors want to set a good example for their employees. The problem that arises, however, is in deciding what is a good example. Some supervisors think that in order to set a good example they must be busy or at least look busy all the time. The result is that the supervisor hoards work that logically should be delegated.

PRINCIPLES OF SUPERVISION BASED ON AUTHORITY

Because the proper use of authority is a key to successful supervision, numerous related principles have been developed. These principles should be viewed as guides to assist the supervisor and not laws to be followed without exception.

The parity principle. The parity principle states that authority and responsibility must coincide. While this principle was implicit in earlier discussions relating to delegation, it was not specifically named. Supervisors must delegate sufficient authority so employees can do their jobs. At the same time, employees can be expected to accept responsibility only for those areas within their authority. In other words, if supervisors make employees responsible for certain actions, then they must give the employees sufficient authority to meet those responsibilities.

The exception principle. The exception principle (also known as management by exception) is closely related to the parity principle. The exception principle states that supervisors should concentrate their efforts on matters that deviate from the normal and let their employees handle routine matters. The idea is that supervisors should not become bogged down with insignificant and routine matters. The exception principle can be abused by incompetent and insecure employees. This happens when employees refer everything to their boss because they are afraid to make a decision. Another problem is the supervisor who continues to make decisions that have supposedly been delegated.

Unity of command. The principle of unity of command states that an employee should have one and only one immediate boss. The difficulty of serving more than one boss has been recognized for thousands of years. Recall the Sermon on the Mount when Jesus said, "No man can serve two masters." Experts have speculated that violation of this principle accounts for almost one third of the human relations problems in industry. This problem occurs when two or more supervisors tell an employee to do different things at the same time. The employee is placed in a no-win situation. Regardless of what the employee does, one supervisor will be dissatisfied. Violation of this principle is usually caused by unclear lines of authority and poor communications.

Scalar principle. The scalar principle states that authority flows one link at a time from the top of the organization to the bottom. The scalar principle is also referred to as the chain of command. Violations of the scalar principle occur when one or more links in the chain of command are bypassed. For example, suppose Jerry goes directly above his immediate boss, Ellen, to her boss, Charlie, for permission to take an early lunch break. Believing the request to be reasonable, Charlie approves it. Later Charlie discovers that the other two people in Jerry's department have also rescheduled their lunch breaks. Thus, the department would be totally vacant from 12:30 to 1:00. Had Ellen not been bypassed, this problem could have easily been avoided. The problem is not that Charlie is incapable of making a good decision, but rather that he does not have the necessary information.

A common misconception is that every action must painfully progress through every link in the scalar chain. The key is to use common sense. If a certain superior has a need to know, that person should be included. On the other hand, if the request is informational in nature, there is usually no need to go through a superior.

Span of control. The span of control refers to the number of employees a supervisor can effectively manage. For years, the span of control was thought to be five to seven. However, practitioners experienced many situations when this did not hold. For example, a floor of 50 punch-press operators all doing the same work would not require 8 to 10 supervisors. Recently the principle of the span of control has been revised to state that a supervisor's span depends on several factors. These factors are complexity of the job, the variety of the jobs, the proximity of the jobs, the quality of the people filling the jobs, and the ability of the supervisor.

While much thought is often given to ensuring that a supervisor's span is not too large, the opposite situation is often overlooked. It is easy for situations to develop in which too few employees report to a supervisor. These situations can lead to an inefficient organization.

Chapter 6

COMMUNICATING WITH EMPLOYEES

Many supervisors know their jobs but have difficulty when it comes to informing others and teaching them what they need to know. They may have adequate decision-making ability and technical competence, but not the necessary communication skills. It has been estimated that communication occupies between 50 to 90 percent of a supervisor's time. It has also been estimated that as much as 70 percent of organizational communications fail to achieve their purpose. Good communication requires time and effort in writing, talking, reading, listening, and interpreting. It represents a definite skill in which every supervisor should attain proficiency. What is *not* communicated can also be vital. Some things are best not said or written, and seldom is it necessary or desirable to communicate everything. Like most things, communication can be excessive, so that the really important messages become lost.

COMMUNICATION AND UNDERSTANDING

The purpose of communication is to transmit information, ideas, or thoughts to someone else. The intent is to achieve *understandability* of the information being conveyed by the person receiving the message.

Telling a fact to another person or sending notice of it, while important, is seldom the only thing involved in communication. There is no genuine communication unless the message is understood. Lack of understanding by the recipient is perhaps the biggest difficulty encountered in communication.

The environment under which a communication is made also influences the understanding of it. *How* a person is told ofen is as important as *what* the person is told. The adage, "Actions speak louder than words," holds true; employees tend to believe and to be influenced not only by what the supervisor says but by what the superior does. A climate of trust and confidence greatly aids communication.

Communication is a two-way process. In order for the process to be effective, information must flow back and forth between the sender and receiver. The flow of information from the receiver to the sender is called feedback. Feedback can be verbal or nonverbal. Limited feedback decreases the time required in the communication process. Unfortunately, it also decreases the accuracy and the degree of confidence the listener has in the accuracy. Thus, feedback takes more time but significantly improves the understanding of the communication.

LISTENING

Listening is the primary method of receiving messages. Unfortunately, most people are not very good listeners. Research has shown that the average person retains only about 25 percent of what is heard. Effective listening is not a natural skill for most people. One factor that influences how well a person listens is the attitude of the listener toward the sender. For example, most people tend to listen more closely to their boss than to their subordinates. Respect for the sender and the belief that the receiver will benefit from the message definitely increase listening retention. For example, how many times have you been introduced to someone but failed to get the person's name because you were preoccupied? Posture, personal mannerisms, and method of speaking can also affect listening retention.

Fortunately, effective listening can be learned. The key to good listening is concentration. One way to concentrate is to anticipate the sender's next point. If the listener is wrong, listening is reinforced because what was said is automatically compared to what was antici-

FIGURE 6–1
Tips for improving your listening skills

1. Stop talking.
   You cannot listen if you are talking.
   Polonius (Hamlet): "Give every man thine ear, but few thy voice."
2. Put the talker at ease.
   Help a person feel free to talk.
   This is often called a permissive environment.
3. Show a talker that you want to listen.
   Look and act interested. Do not read your mail while someone talks.
   Listen to understand rather than to oppose.
4. Remove distractions.
   Don't doodle, tap, or shuffle papers.
   Will it be quieter if you shut the door?
5. Empathize with talkers.
   Try to help yourself see the other person's point of view.
6. Be patient.
   Allow plenty of time. Do not interrupt a talker.
   Don't start for the door or walk away.
7. Hold your temper.
   An angry person takes the wrong meaning from words.
8. Go easy on argument and criticism.
   This puts people on the defensive, and they may clam up or become
   angry.
   Do not argue. Even if you win, you lose.
9. Ask questions.
   This encourages a talker and shows that you are listening.
   It helps to develop points further.
10. Stop talking.
   This is first and last, because all other guides depend on it. You cannot
   do an effective listening job while you are talking.

Source: Keith Davis, *Human Relations at Work*, 5th ed. (New York: McGraw-Hill, 1978) p. 387.

pated. If the listener is correct, the learning is reinforced. Another way is to make mental summaries. When the sender stops or pauses, the listener should summarize mentally the key points that have been made. Figure 6–1 lists several tips for effective listening.

Effective listening generally assumes that receivers are interested in what senders have to say. But if receivers are not interested, what can senders do? It is always helpful for supervisors to show how particular communications affect the receivers. Sometimes, when people receive a message, they wonder, "Why do I need to know this?" If supervisors address this question at the start, they are more likely to raise receivers' interest level. Eliminating unnecessary messages also can help to raise receiver interest.

FIGURE 6–2
Interpretations of the word *fix*

An Englishman visits America and is completely awed by the many ways we use the word *fix*. For example:

1. His host asks him how he'd like his drink fixed. He meant *mixed.*
2. His hostess calls to the guests to finish their drinks because dinner is all fixed. She means *prepared.*
3. As he prepares to leave, he discovers that he has a flat tire and calls a repairman who says he'll fix it immediately. He means *repair.*
4. On the way home, he is given a ticket for speeding When he calls his host, the host says, "Don't worry, I'll fix it." He means *nullify.*
5. At the office the next day, he comments on the cost of living in America and one of his cohorts says, "It's hard to make ends meet on a fixed income." He means *steady* or *unchanging.*
6. Later, he remarks that he doesn't know what to do with his college diploma. A colleague says, "I'll fix it on the wall for you." He means *attach.*
7. He has an argument with a co-worker. The latter says, "I'll fix you." He means *seek revenge.*
8. Another of his cohorts remarks that she is in a hell of a fix. She means *condition or situation.*
9. He meets a friend at this boarding house who offers to fix him up with a girl. You know what that means.

PERCEPTION AND SEMANTICS

Perception refers to how people view situations. Experience, personality, and method of communication affect a person's perception. Because these factors differ, each person's perception is unique. This explains why two people can view the same situation in entirely different ways. For example, a message may be received and interpreted in an entirely different manner than the way in which it was intended. Supervisors should never assume that their actions and words are going to be perceived exactly as they were intended. In fact, it is probably safer to assume that they will not be. Feedback, which was discussed earlier, is the most effective method of reducing differences in perception.

Semantics is the study of the meaning of words and symbols. Words have meaning only in terms of how they are perceived and understood by people. Facial expressions, hand gestures, and voice inflection influence the understanding of words. Two general problems tend to arise in semantics that influence the communication process. First, some words and phrases can have multiple interpretations. For example, as shown in Figure 6–2, the word *fix* can be used in many ways. In addition, some groups of people in particular situations develop their own technical language that may not be understood by outsiders. For example, doctors, lawyers, government and military employees often use abbreviations and acronyms that only they understand.

Since words are the most common method of communication, they must be carefully chosen and clearly defined. Again, the use of feedback can reduce the failures in communication that result from semantics.

THE GRAPEVINE

The grapevine is the communication system that results from the informal organization. Superimposed upon the formal organization, the informal organization nurtures and carries much important information. As a quick and highly effective distributor of "news," it is not always accurate, but it enjoys a high degree of acceptance. Employees want information about their jobs, their fellow employees, future company plans, their chances for advancement, and hundreds of other items. The grapevine thrives on these inherent desires.

The smart supervisor uses the grapevine as a supplement to formal communication. Supervisors should be extremely careful not to attack everything in the grapevine because their credibility can be damaged. This is especially true if the information or even a portion of it is accurate. If a supervisor hears information in the grapevine and knows that it is true, a meeting should be called to acknowledge the truthfulness of the information. If the information is false, the supervisor should call a meeting to correct the information. The key is to use the grapevine rather than to fight it.

HANDLING MEETINGS

From time to time, the typical supervisor holds meetings with group members to solve common problems or to give, get, or exchange information. There are certain practices that can make the most of any such meeting. Most meetings should have a specific agenda that should be closely followed. If the agenda is given in advance to each of the people who are going to participate in the meeting, these people can then be prepared to discuss their views on the agenda items. A specific time period should also be allocated for the meeting. All of these suggestions keep the meeting from dragging out and accomplishing

FIGURE 6–3
Guides for conducting effective meetings

1. A specific agenda should be prepared in advance and given to each participant in the meeting.
2. A specific time period should be established for the meeting.
3. The meeting should begin and end on time.
4. Each member should be encouraged to participate.
5. Certain members should not be allowed to dominate the meeting.
6. The supervisor should actively participate in, but not dominate, the meeting.
7. Lengthy discussions by one member should be politely curtailed.
8. Written summaries of the results of the meeting should be given to each participant as quickly as possible.

very little. Each person at the meeting should be encouraged to participate. Attendees should be encouraged to ask questions, raise objections, and relate what they like and do not like about the subject at hand. At the same time, the supervisor should not allow certain members to dominate the meeting. Lengthy discussions by one member should be politely curtailed. The supervisor should lead the meeting and also actively participate in the discussion but should be careful not to dominate the meeting. The meeting should begin and end at its scheduled time. Written summaries on the results of the meeting should be given to each participant as quickly as possible. Figure 6–3 summarizes these guides for conducting effective meetings.

GIVING INSTRUCTIONS

Another common situation that all supervisors face and that requires effective communication skills is giving instructions. How often have you given what you considered to be perfectly clear instructions only to have them incorrectly interpreted? This is especially a problem for supervisors since they spend a significant portion of their time giving instructions. Naturally the manner in which instructions are communicated is critical. In order to be effective, a supervisor must learn how to give instructions to people. The following suggestions should be helpful.

1 The supervisor should employ a pleasant attitude when giving instructions. Instructions given in a friendly manner are most likely to be met with friendly cooperation.

2. The acronym, "KISS," is applicable when giving instructions. "KEEP IT SIMPLE, STUPID." Instructions should not be overly long and complex. In order to provide clear, concise instructions, the supervisor should plan and organize thoughts before giving the instructions.

3. The supervisor should explain not only what to do but also explain why the instructions are being given.

4. The supervisor should ask people to explain what they are going to do as a result of receiving the instructions and should *not* ask if they understand what was said.

5. The supervisor should follow up by checking to see if the instructions are being followed. A word of caution should be given here: Too much checking can demotivate people. There is a delicate balance between too much and too little checking.

IMPROVING YOUR COMMUNICATION SKILLS

Failure by the supervisor to develop good communication skills—verbal, written, and nonverbal—can also cause many communication breakdowns. Many supervisors use statements such as "I am not a public speaker" or "I never could write very well" as excuses to explain their weaknesses in these areas. The desire to be a supervisor should carry with it the desire to improve one's weaknesses in these areas. Some concise guides are presented below that relate to improving a supervisor's verbal, written, and nonverbal skills.

Verbal skills. Most people have little trouble in carrying on a conversation when it is a one-on-one situation. A supervisor does a great deal of one-on-one communicating when giving job instructions, disciplining employees, answering questions, and communicating with the boss. The following are some helpful hints for improving one-on-one verbal skills:

1. Determine in advance the purpose of the conversation.

2. Organize your thoughts before you begin talking. Some supervisors tend to talk on and on with little organization to their thoughts.

3. Listen to what the other party has to say.

4. Ask for feedback from friends about their perception of your one-on-one verbal skills. A word of caution must be given here: Don't be hurt if they point out weaknesses. Learn from the feedback.

5. If possible, tape record yourself during a one-on-one session. Listen to your voice; eliminate such phrases as "you know" and other personalized expressions that detract from your communication effectiveness.

Writing skills. The supervisor's writing skills are most frequently used when communicating within the formal organization. Memos, written disciplinary actions, and reports require effective writing skills. Some hints for improving your writing skills are listed below:

1. Outline your thoughts before putting them into writing. An outline gives you the opportunity to look at the organization of your presentation. Does the presentation flow smoothly? Are there logical transitions between major points?
2. Get feedback on your writing. Again, don't take any negative feedback personally. Learn from the feedback.
3. Practice writing whenever you can.
4. Read periodicals that relate to supervision. After reading an article, analyze whether it was logically organized and think about what you would have done differently.

Chapter 7

MOTIVATING EMPLOYEES

"Nobody wants to work the way they did in the good old days." "Half the problems we have around here are due to a lack of personal motivation." "Workers just don't seem to care." Statements such as these are often expressed by today's supervisors. However, motivating employees is not a new problem. Much of the pioneering work in the field of management, which took place early in this century, was concerned with motivation. One can go further back to Biblical times and find other examples dealing with motivational problems.

WHAT IS MOTIVATION?

Numerous definitions can be found for the word *motivation*. Often included in these definitions are such words as *aim, desire, end, impulse, intention, objective,* and *purpose*. The word *motivation* actually comes from the Latin word *movere* (to move.). In today's organizations, motivation means getting a person to exert a high degree of effort. In other words, a motivated employee is one who tries hard. The key to motivation, then, is getting employees to want to do a job. In this light, motivation is not something that the supervisor does *to* an employee. Rather, motivation is something that must come from within the employee. The supervisor can, however, create an environment that encourages motivation on the part of employees. This is the context in which a supervisor "motivates" employees.

WHY PEOPLE BEHAVE AS THEY DO

Every supervisor knows that some people are easier to motivate than others. Why is this true? Are some people simply born more motivated than others? No person is exactly like any other person. Each individual has a unique personality and makeup. Thus, because people are different, it only stands to reason that different factors are required to motivate different people. Yet, many supervisors expect all employees to react in a similar manner. Each person is the result of a special mix consisting of physical conditions, ancestry, home life, education, experiences, work, and beliefs. Whatever a person says, does, or thinks is due to a reason that is meaningful to that person. Certain words and actions may be meaningless to others, but this occurs because others do not view the actions through the eyes of the doer. At some time or other, most supervisors are puzzled by the lack of enthusiasm or initiative of some employees. If supervisors could determine why this behavior exists, they would have a greater understanding of such employees and might be able to modify unproductive behavior.

When attempting to understand human behavior, the supervisor should always remember that people do things for a reason. The reason may be imaginary, inaccurate, distorted, or unjustifiable, but it is real to the person. The reason, whatever it may be, must be identified before the supervisor can understand the person's behavior. All too often a supervisor disregards an employee's reason for a certain behavior as being unrealistic or based on inaccurate information. This is the supervisor who responds by saying, "I don't care what he thinks; that is not the way it is!" This supervisor will probably never understand why employees behave as they do.

The supervisor who knows what an employee is striving for, and why, can better understand that person. When a sought-for goal is being achieved, feelings of pride, satisfaction, and confidence are evident in the person's behavior. In contrast, if the goal is not being achieved, the accompanying feelings may be those of futility, negativism, and a sense of alienation from society. Reactions to successful or unsuccessful goal attainment, however, will differ among people. Some react to success by feeling compelled to reach for higher and more difficult goals; others will be satisfied with what they have achieved. People also react to failure differently. Some do not accept failure when certain goals are not readily reached; others will withdraw or just give up.

Another consideration in understanding human behavior is the concept of the self-fulfilling prophecy. Also known as the "Pygmalion effect," this concept refers to the tendency of an employee to live up to the supervisor's expectations. Closely related to the Pygmalion effect is the tendency of the supervisor to see an employee's behavior as the supervisor wants to see it. In other words, if a supervisor expects an employee to succeed, the employee usually will succeed. Of course the opposite is also true. If a supervisor expects an employee to fail, the employee usually will fail. Thus, supervisors' attitudes toward their employees can have a significant impact on the employees' performance.

THEORY X AND THEORY Y

Douglas McGregor has described two divergent attitudes that leaders (supervisors in our case) may have. These attitudes are called Theory X and Theory Y. Theory X maintains that the average employee dislikes work and will do whatever possible to avoid it. Theory Y states that people like work and that it comes as naturally as rest and play. (Figure 7–1 outlines in greater detail Theory X and Theory Y.) McGregor

FIGURE 7–1
Assumptions about people

Theory X

1. The average person has an inherent dislike of work and will avoid it whenever possible.
2. Because of this human characteristic of dislike of work, most people must be coerced, controlled, directed, threatened with punishment to get them to put forth adequate effort toward the achievement of organizational objectives.
3. The average person prefers to be directed, wishes to avoid responsibility, has relatively little ambition, wants security above all.

Theory Y

1. The expenditure of physical and mental effort in work is as natural as play or rest.
2. External control and the threat of punishment are not the only means for bringing about effort toward organizational objectives. People will exercise self-direction and self-control in the service of objectives to which they are committed.
3. Commitment to objectives is a function of the rewards associated with their achievement.
4. The average person learns, under proper conditions, not only to accept but to seek responsibility.
5. The capacity to exercise a relatively high degree of imagination, ingenuity, and creativity in the solution of organizational problems is widely, not narrowly, distributed in the population.
6. Under the conditions of modern industrial life, the intellectual potentialities of the average person are only partially utilized.

Source: Adapted from Douglas McGregor, *The Human Side of Enterprise* (New York: McGraw-Hill, 1960). Copyright by McGraw-Hill, Inc. Used with permission of McGraw-Hill Book Company, 1960, pp. 33–34 and 47–48.

maintained that many leaders basically subscribe to either Theory X or Theory Y and that they behave accordingly. Thus, a leader subscribing to Theory X would more than likely use a much more autocratic style of supervision than a leader who believes in Theory Y assumptions. The real contribution coming from McGregor's work was the suggestion that a leader's attitude toward human nature has a large influence on how the person behaves as a leader.

HUMAN NEEDS

All humans have needs—physical, psychological, and social. The desire to satisfy them conditions their behavior. What needs particular individuals have and how they strive to satisfy them will vary because of individual differences.

Psychologist A. H. Maslow has identified five basic needs: (1) physical, (2) safety, (3) social, (4) esteem, and (5) self-actualization. These are diagrammed and identified in Figure 7–2.

Maslow believed that only one level of needs serves as the primary motivation of a person at any given time. Furthermore, he believed that humans start with the lower order needs of the hierarchy and move up the hierarchy one level at a time as the needs become satisfied. Thus, the physical needs tend to dominate all other needs until they are substantially satisfied. Once the physical needs have been satisfied, the safety needs become dominant in the need structure. This process

FIGURE 7–2
The hierarchy of human needs

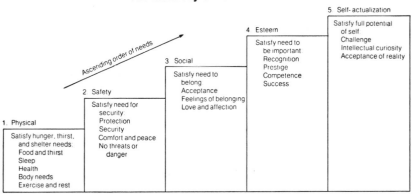

continues with different needs emerging as each respective level of needs is satisfied. Most employees are able to satisfy physical and safety needs; fewer satisfy affection needs, and fewer still, esteem needs. Only a select few are so fortunate as to satisfy self-actualization needs.

Although the needs of the majority of the people are arranged in the sequence shown in Figure 7–2, differences in the sequence can occur depending on an individual's learning experiences, culture, and social upbringing.

As far as motivation is concerned, the thrust of this theory is that a satisfied need is not a motivator. It is important for the supervisor to identify the unsatisfied needs of employees and to make it possible for them to satisfy these needs through their jobs. Only then will employees be enthusiastic about their work and motivated to perform it.

THE IMPORTANCE OF JOB DESIGN

Frederick Herzberg has developed a theory of motivation that deals primarily with motivation through job design. Herzberg's theory is based on the belief that the factors that demotivate or turn off employees are different from those factors that motivate or turn on employees. Herzberg maintains that the factors which tend to demotivate employees are usually associated with the work environment. These factors include such things as job status, interpersonal relations with supervisors and peers, the style of supervision the person receives, company policy and administration, job security, working conditions, pay, and aspects of personal life that are affected by the work situation. Herzberg refers to these factors as *hygiene* or *maintenance* factors. These terms were chosen because these factors are perceived as being preventative in nature. In other words, they will not produce motivation but can prevent motivation from occurring. Thus, proper attention to hygiene factors is a necessary but not sufficient condition for motivation. For example, Herzberg contends that pay will not motivate a person (at least for more than a short period of time) but it can certainly demotivate a person.

According to Herzberg, those factors that motivate people are factors related to the work itself as opposed to the work environment. These factors are called motivators and include achievement, recognition, responsibility, advancement, and the challenges of the job. Herzberg

FIGURE 7–3
Hygiene-motivator factors

Hygiene factors *Relate to the environment*	Motivator factors *Relate to the job itself*
Policies and administration	Achievement
Supervision	Recognition
Working conditions	Challenging work
Interpersonal relations	Increased responsibility
Personal life	Advancement
Money, status, security	Personal growth

maintains that true motivation occurs only when both the motivators and hygiene factors are present. At best, proper attention to the hygiene factors will keep an individual from being dissatisfied but will not make the individual motivated. Figure 7–3 lists some examples of hygiene and motivator factors.

As a solution to motivation problems, Herzberg developed an approach called job enrichment. Unlike job enlargement or job rotation, job enrichment involves upgrading the job by adding motivator factors. (Job enlargement merely involves giving a worker more of a similar type of operation to perform. Job rotation is the practice of periodically rotating job assignments.) Designing jobs that provide for meaningful work, achievement, recognition, responsibility, advancement, and growth is the key to job enrichment.

WHAT CAN THE SUPERVISOR DO?

There are several things that a supervisor can do to affect employee motivation. Some of the most useful of these are:

Make the work interesting.

Relate rewards to performance.

Provide valued rewards.

Treat employees as individuals.

Encourage participation and cooperation.

Provide accurate and timely feedback.

Make the work interesting. Supervisors should carefully examine each job under their control. They should constantly ask, "Can this job be enriched in order to make the job more challenging?" There is a limit to the extent that people can be expected to perform satisfactorily on very routine tasks. Doing the same simple task over and over again every minute of the workday can quickly lead to employee apathy and boredom.

There is a tendency on the part of many supervisors to say, "This job just can't be enriched." However, more often than not, jobs can be enriched without causing a total reorganization within the department. Use secretaries as an example. How often are secretaries treated as if they are incapable of doing anything other than typing and maybe a little filing? The result is that usually they become bored and demotivated. However, with a little planning and thought, this same job can be easily enriched. Secretaries can be assigned responsibilities such as responding to certain correspondence, opening and sorting the mail, making appointments, and so forth. The key is to make the job challenging and interesting.

Relate rewards to performance. There are many reasons why supervisors are reluctant to relate rewards directly to performance. First and foremost, it is much easier to give everyone an equal pay raise. Usually this approach involves less hassle and requires very little justification. A second reason may be because of the union contract. Union contracts generally require that everyone doing the same job be paid the same wage. In other instances, organizational policy dictates that pay raises conform to certain guidelines unrelated to performance. Even in these instances, however, there usually are rewards other than pay that can be related to performance. These might include the assignment of preferred tasks or some type of formal recognition. The costs of failing to relate rewards to performance are great. Not only are the low performers not motivated to do more, but the high performers are motivated to do less. Every supervisor should strive to relate rewards directly to performance.

Provide valued rewards. Most supervisors never stop to give any thought to what types of rewards are most valued by employees. Usually supervisors, like all managers, tend to think of pay as the only reward at their disposal. Most supervisors truly believe that they have nothing to say about what rewards are offered. The common belief is that these decisions are made by upper management. However, there are many other types of rewards that might be highly valued by employees. Being assigned to work on a certain project or being assigned a new piece of equipment represents rewards that might be highly valued by employees. The important thing is for supervisors to know what rewards are at their disposal and to know what the employees value.

Treat employees as individuals. As discussed earlier, different people have different needs. Different people want different things from their jobs. To treat everyone the same ignores these differences. In today's highly impersonal world, there is an increasing tendency to treat employees as if they are computer numbers. Most people like to receive special attention and to be treated as individuals. Such attention raises people's self-esteem and makes them feel a part of the organization. Treating employees as individuals usually results in more frequent and candid interaction between the supervisors and the employees. In such a climate, employees naturally feel more like talking over their ideas with the supervisor.

Encourage participation and cooperation. All people like to feel a part of their surroundings. Similarly, people like to feel that they contribute to their surroundings. It is also natural for them to be committed to decisions in which they have participated. The motivational benefits of true employee participation are undoubtedly high. Yet, in spite of all the potential benefits, many supervisors do little to encourage participation. Take for instance the familiar suggestion box. As soon as employees discover that their suggestions are not taken seriously, the suggestion box becomes a collection point for obscene jokes. Employees who make several worthwhile suggestions to no avail soon quit making suggestions. The point is that active participation requires commitment on the part of supervisors. This does not just naturally happen. Employees must genuinely feel that their participation is valued.

Closely related to participation is the need to sufficiently explain the reasons for certain actions. Employees naturally are more motivated to do something when they understand why the action is being taken.

Provide accurate and timely feedback. People do not like to be in the dark concerning their performance. In fact, a negative performance review may be better than no review. In this situation, the person will at least know what must be done to improve. A lack of feedback usually produces frustration in employees. This frustration often has a negative impact on employee performance. Providing accurate and timely feedback involves more than just regularly scheduled performance appraisals (which are discussed in depth in the next chapter). This also involves providing informal feedback on a regular basis.

It is easy for supervisors to fall into the trap of taking too much for granted. No one likes to be taken for granted. A simple verbal or written statement of appreciation can go a long way. A potential danger, however, is to become overly complimentary to the point that it loses impact.

Criticisms, if not properly used, can negatively affect motivation. Normally criticisms should not be voiced in front of others, but rather should be communicated in private. Unfortunately, there is often a strong natural tendency to lash out verbally at a subordinate when a mistake is made. The employee can be turned off very quickly by such actions. It is important to realize that the feedback provided should include both the positive and negative happenings. All too often supervisors focus only on the negative. The goal is for the employee to know at all times exactly where he or she stands.

Chapter 8

EMPLOYEE DEVELOPMENT

One of the prime objectives of supervision is to encourage employees to develop their full potential. People come to an organization wanting to contribute, but most of them need help to do so. Employees are going to develop to some degree and in some way whether a formal development program exists or not. Proper attention should be given to employee development to ensure that this development is done in the best possible manner and on an orderly basis.

THE SUPERVISOR AND DEVELOPMENT EFFORTS

Many organizations have a director of development or training, although the activities directed by this management member vary from organization to organization. Usually they include the determination of training needs; the supply of training facilities—books, rooms, and exams; the provision of expertise in training methods; and the handling of classes and group meetings. In some cases, however, developmental efforts are managed by outsiders. Either the employees are sent to a nearby school or university, or an instructor is hired to handle certain courses on company premises (in-plant programs).

Supervisors usually provide much of the in-house training. When group members need help in performing their work, it is the supervisor to whom they turn. Likewise, it is the supervisor who conditions the work environment, motivates the employee to learn how to do the work, and helps the employee gain personal satisfaction from being able to perform the work successfully. Thus, the supervisor occupies a key position in making the developmental efforts effective. It should be noted that development work is an everyday, continuing effort. Unless it is planned and conducted on a regular basis, it exists in name only.

THE NEED FOR EMPLOYEE DEVELOPMENT

Usually it is not difficult to demonstrate the need for employee training. The evidence is everywhere: lack of job enthusiasm, low productivity, numerous employee complaints, high-waste rates. While there are diverse reasons for such conditions, usually they can be improved with proper training. If necessary, a training program can be keyed directly to minimizing a specific undesirable situation.

The primary need is to make employees able to contribute more effectively to the accomplishment of stated goals. These goals may be varied, but related, such as to accomplish tasks properly within a specified time, to be good members of a team effort, or to obtain genuine satisfaction from performing the work. There is also a need for retraining employees to meet the requirements of a new product or process, to correct current activities that are being improperly performed, and to improve job performance. Training is especially important to ensure that faulty practices are minimized and do not become the accepted method for performing the work.

ORIENTING THE NEW EMPLOYEE

Orientation is concerned with introducing the new employee to the organization and to the job. During the hiring process, most people learn the general aspects of the job and the organization. This usually includes such things as the job duties, working conditions, and pay. After the employee is hired, the orientation program begins. In large organizations, the supervisor and the personnel department usually share the orientation responsibilities. If the organization has no personnel department, or only a small one, the supervisor is generally responsible for conducting the orientation. Figure 8–1 summarizes information that should be covered in an orientation program.

FIGURE 8–1
Information to be covered in orientation by the supervisor if there is no personnel department

For the organization, include:

1. The objectives and philosophy of the organization.
2. An explanation of the organization's operations, the levels of authority, and how they relate.
3. A brief history of the organization.
4. What is expected of the new employee: attitude, reliability, initiative, emotional maturity, and personal appearance.
5. Job functions and responsibilities.
6. Rules, regulations, policies, and procedures.
7. Why the organization needs the new employee.
8. City, state, and federal laws, if applicable.
9. Functions of management.
10. Telephone techniques.

For the new employee, include:

1. A welcome.
2. Introduction to the department and fellow workers.
3. General office practice and business etiquette.
4. Skill training.
5. Job responsibilities.
6. Performance evaluation criteria.
7. Promotional opportunities.
8. Conditions of employment: punctuality, attendance, conduct, hours of work, overtime, termination.
9. Pay procedures.
10. Benefits: salary, job security, insurance, recreational facilities, employee activities, rest periods, holidays, vacation, sick leave, leave of absence, tuition refund, pension.
11. Safety and fire prevention.
12. Personnel policies.
13. Techniques for learning.
14. Encouragement.

Source: Adapted from Joan Holland and Theodore Curtis, "Orientation of New Employees," *Handbook of Modern Personnel Administration,* ed. Joseph Famularo (New York: McGraw-Hill, 1972), pp. 23–24, 23–25.

Too many supervisors give little, if any, attention to the orientation process. A poor orientation program can quickly sour a new employee's attitude about the job and the organization. Most people come to a new job with a positive attitude. However, if a new employee is made to feel unimportant by the lack of an orientation program, this attitude can quickly change. If a formal orientation program is not possible, new employees will receive informal orientation either from their fellow workers or from the supervisor. Good, well-planned orientation programs reduce job-learning time, improve attendance, and lead to higher output. Thus, effective supervisors plan and conduct good orientation programs.

TRAINING EXPERIENCES

Training involves the acquisition of skills, concepts, rules, or attitudes in order to increase the performance of employees. Training efforts require adequate planning. The most successful programs are shaped from the beginning by the specific training objectives to be achieved.

A fundamental aspect of all training is creating within the trainee an intense desire to learn. In the final analysis, all learning is self-learning. The training program provides the opportunity to learn, but if the trainee does not want to learn or is not willing to make the required effort, the learning will not be effective.

Participants in a training program should be selected primarily on the basis of the requirements of the job and the needs and capabilities of the employee. Education, experience, personality, psychological needs, and potential for promotion can affect the suitability of individual trainees.

Training sessions may be held in a number of different locations, but for convenience they can be classified as either on-the-job or off-the-job programs. On-the-job training features individualized face-to-face instruction that takes place at the regular work place whenever the instructor believes it is needed. The supervisor gives much or all of the on-the-job training. Off-the-job training is usually used when it is less costly and quicker to communicate the training material to several members of a group. The number of trainees to be handled, the type of material, and past practices are considerations in deciding which type of program to use.

HOW TO SUCCESSFULLY TRAIN OPERATIVE EMPLOYEES

A good procedure to follow when training employees is shown in Figure 8–2. No one can force a trainee to learn; the trainee must want to do so. Instructors or supervisors can obtain information about the employee's ambitions, likes, and dislikes; point out the advantages of learning to perform a particular job; and give examples of successful training. All this can be used to develop the employee's interest in wanting to learn.

The training method of breaking down difficult work into a series of relatively simple operations, showing how to perform each operation, and then tying the operations together is a rational approach that shows quickly and exactly what is needed to do the work. Special attention should be given to the key points—those portions of the job which require a special knack or skill. It is at the key points that the learner is most likely to have difficulty.

Regardless of the type of training that is used, there are several common pitfalls a supervisor should avoid in order to make employees' training experiences more meaningful. Failure to let employees know how well they are doing is a common pitfall. Too many supervisors tell people "I'll let you know if you aren't doing the job right." However, people also want to know when they are doing the job right. Feedback regarding progress is critical to effective learning. Setting standards of performance for trainees and measuring their performance against the standards encourages learning.

Lack of positive reinforcement is a common error in training. When employees are praised for doing a job correctly, then they are likely to be motivated to do it correctly again. Too many supervisors only point out mistakes. Praise and recognition of trainees can be a very effective means of teaching.

"Practice makes perfect" is very applicable to the learning process. Too many supervisors try to explain the job quickly and then expect employees to do it perfectly the first time. Having trainees perform a particular job or explaining how they would perform a job maintains their concentration and facilitates learning. Repeating a job or task several times also helps. Learning is always helped by practice and repetition.

Frequently, supervisors have preconceived and inaccurate ideas about what certain people or groups of people can or can't do. A supervisor

FIGURE 8-2
Five steps in training for skill acquisition

1. Get the trainee ready to learn.

2. Break down the work into components
   and identify the key points.

3. Demonstrate the approved way the work
   is to be performed.

4. Let the trainee perform the work.

5. Put trainee on his own gradually.

FIGURE 8–3
Conditions for effective learning

1. Acceptance that all people can learn.
2. The individual must be motivated to learn.
3. Learning is an active process, not passive.
4. Normally, the learner must have guidance.
5. Appropriate materials for sequential learning must be provided: hands-on experiences, cases, problems, discussion, reading.
6. Time must be provided to practice the learning; to internalize; to give confidence.
7. Learning methods, if possible, should be varied to avoid boredom.
8. The learner must secure satisfaction from the learning.
9. The learner must get reinforcement of the correct behavior.
10. Standards of performance should be set for the learner.
11. A recognition that there are different levels of learning and that these take different times and methods.

Source: Reproduced by special permission from Leslie This and Gordon Lippitt, "Learning Theories and Training," *Training and Development Journal,* April 1966. Copyright 1966 by the American Society for Training and Development, Inc.

should realize that different people learn at different rates. Some learn rapidly and some learn more slowly. The pace of the training should be adjusted to the trainee. A supervisor shouldn't expect everyone to pick the job up right away. Also, if a person is not a fast learner, this does not mean that the person will always be a poor performer. The supervisor should take the attitude that all people can learn and want to learn. Figure 8–3 summarizes several conditions for effective learning. A supervisor should attempt to develop these conditions for all trainees.

SUPERVISORY DEVELOPMENT PROGRAMS

Of all the training programs an organization could have, a supervisory program is generally recognized as one of the most important. To be fully effective, it should be designed by the supervisors, not for them. The best supervisory programs consider typical everyday problems supervisors are called upon to solve, and tentative answers to them are developed and discussed by participants in the program. Remember, supervisors are people of action who are not accustomed to listening to someone expound knowledge, much of which is theoretical and from which they cannot perceive immediate benefits.

As with all developmental efforts, the objectives for supervisory training programs must be clearly stated. The program should stress learning by means of activities designed to develop insight and give applicable knowledge. It should also be flexible, since learning situations are dynamic and the supervisor's work does not remain constant. The question of which supervisors should attend the training sessions brings up issues regarding the course content. For example, a supervisor who has attended many training sessions probably will profit most from an advanced level course, whereas a new supervisor probably should have a course that explains basics. It is wasteful to subject all supervisors to the same general type of course again and again. True, some repetition is desirable, and something new is picked up each time a member is exposed to such a program; but an arrangement should be developed that will avoid unnecessary repetition and be effective for all participants.

Closely allied with the question of who should attend what sessions are the needs of the supervisors. An evaluation of each supervisor's major assets and limitations is recommended so that a reasonably good idea of the possible gain from a course can be determined. Such an evaluation might take the form of a well-planned personal interview with supervisors to determine their needs and discover their preferences.

Chapter 9

BUILDING TEAM EFFORT

Getting work accomplished effectively and under conditions satisfactory to all concerned is the dual task of supervision. This can best be accomplished when the employees have a high degree of loyalty, interact well with each other, and have high-performance goals. Supervisors should consciously attempt to build this type of feeling within their work groups. Developing this type of work group is referred to as "building team effort" or "developing team spirit."

THE INFLUENCE OF THE WORK GROUP

Whether a group of employees brought together by organizational activities will develop into an effective team depends upon several factors. First, it must be recognized that the behavior of the group is an entity in itself; it is not simply the sum of the behaviors of the individual members. This means that the supervisor must sometimes deal differently with the group than with the individuals of the group.

Second, members of a group tend to forego some individual desires in order to conform to the wishes and behavior of the group. Although group members may do this willingly, they recognize there is pressure from the group to conform to its wishes. People who become group members no longer stand alone and independently evaluate and decide issues. As group members, they are a part of something larger that in some measure not only replaces but encompasses personal behavior. Now the function is to cooperate with the group, to be an active part of it, to contribute to it, and to help realize the group's goals. In these ways, group members make it possible for a team to take shape, to develop team spirit, and to achieve goals not otherwise possible.

Third, a group has a personality that is stronger than that of any single individual member and reflects the joint behavior and outlook of its members. The group has a conscience that overshadows the conscience of individual members. This is acceptable to most people because they usually want to belong to the team rather than be considered somewhat odd by fellow employees.

A group norm is an understanding among the members of a group concerning how they should behave. For example, some work groups play jokes or tricks on all new employees. Another example is the establishment of certain performance or production standards that all group members are not expected to exceed. Unfortunately, these standards of production may be below what management feels they should be. Therefore, the supervisor should constantly be aware of the influence that the group can have on the actions of the individual group members.

GROUP DYNAMICS

The term *group dynamics* refers to interactions among a group of people who depend upon one another and share fundamental ideas or activities. Several elements must be present in order for group dynamics to be effective. Group members must have (1) a common goal, (2) mutual like and trust for each other, and (3) knowledge of the exchanges involved in terms of such things as rewards, results, and cost. Unanimity of purpose is essential. Each member cannot seek individual special interests, for to do so places the group in jeopardy. The affection and trust members have for one another provide friendly relationships that encourage the free exchange of giving and receiving. Communication also is enhanced by good group dynamics.

HOW A TEAM DEVELOPS

When people begin to work together, cliques tend to form. Certain people are drawn together by common interests. Likes and dislikes of certain employees for other employees emerge. Efforts are made by certain employees to get to know other employees. Recognition of the status and authority of some members becomes evident, and information alignment based upon them usually is made. Those who communicate well and are able to accomplish the desired goals will gain stature and be granted positions of leadership. However, the interaction among group members is continuous. The forces of attraction and rejection constantly operate within the group, and the alignments of members may change over time.

While the influence or personal qualities of one group member may attract some members, the same characteristics may be considered ample justification for rejection by other members. Such actions are not necessarily rational but depend upon the particular case and its individual circumstances. In any group at a given time, there are typically certain members who seek each other out, work together, and talk together. And there are also "isolates"—those who are not fully accepted as members. They are isolates for any of a number of reasons, but mainly because they prefer to be alone, they have a deep dislike for status and authority, or they reject the group's work behavior.

A team's spirit and productivity are inherently affected by the work situation. The chances are usually best for achieving a strong team effort when there is a single work activity. A common purpose and mutual interests tend to promote togetherness and the sharing of ways to obtain various group goals. The size of the group also makes a difference. Several small groups are usually preferred to one large group because the smaller ones expedite personal contact and exchanges among members. Further, needless red tape in accomplishing the goal is minimized.

In general, when group members support and assist one another on their own, the group has become a team. Further indications that the group is a team are evidence of a common front against outsiders, a free exchange of members' ideas, and kidding among members. Team members highly value the opportunity to associate with fellow members. Team members like to be around fellow team members, to see what they are doing, to talk with them, and to share hopes and ambitions. When these conditions are evident, it is fairly certain that an effective team has developed.

WHAT CAN A SUPERVISOR DO TO BUILD A TEAM?

What can the supervisor do to encourage the development of a team? Basically, supervisors take measures that indirectly make team formation possible. Certainly they cannot order that a team be formed, and they can do little in a direct way to force team development. The changes required to make the group a team must come from the members themselves.

The role of the supervisor is to spark interest in achieving team status and to provide the environment that will encourage such a change to take place. Figure 9–1 shows four ways the supervisor can encourage

FIGURE 9–1
Guidelines for developing team development

1. Establish a friendly and fair working environment.

MUTUAL GOALS
COMBINING of ABILITIES
SHARED RESPONSIBILITY
VOICE in DECISION MAKING
GOOD COMMUNICATION
SENSE of ACHIEVEMENT
PERSONAL JOB SATISFACTION

2. Encourage and listen
   to ideas from group members.

I THINK YOUR PLAN IS A GOOD ONE! I'M GLAD YOU BROUGHT IT TO MY ATTENTION.

3. Demonstrate by your actions that you see issues
   not only from the supervisory viewpoint but also
   from the members' viewpoint.

MANAGER

SUGGESTION BOX

4. Gain acceptance
   into the team of employees.

OUR LEADER

team development. First, the supervisor must establish a working environment that is considered to be fair and friendly. This cannot be done by the supervisor alone. All levels of management must contribute. However, if this environment is not established in the supervisor's work unit, the efforts of higher levels of management will be wasted. The group members must believe that all decisions reached are fair.

Second, participation by the employees in working out changes and keeping them informed about what is taking place also helps build a team spirit. The supervisor should encourage members to believe that they belong, inform them of the problems to be solved, and let them help in determining equitable answers.

The third way that team development can be encouraged is by demonstrating that the supervisor can see things from the group's point of view. The effective supervisor also attempts to see and understand issues from the employees' point of view. However, the supervisor needs to be careful here. A supervisor who is always siding with the employees and taking an attitude of "It's us against them" can create a negative environment. The point is *not* to side with employees against management but to attempt to understand the issues from the employees' point of view.

The fourth suggestion is for the supervisor to strive to gain acceptance as the group's leader. The supervisor does not want to be viewed as an outsider who orders everyone around. Certainly, a supervisor has formal authority that has been delegated from higher levels of management. However, formal authority does not guarantee effective supervision.

INCREASING THE TEAM'S PRODUCTIVITY

The successful supervisor learns to adapt as changes occur in the behavior of group members and group goals are modified. An all-out effort is made to identify and improve goals by working with the members. Proper materials and good equipment are supplied. Complaints are listened to, and the corrective action, when warranted, is taken without delay.

A team with a worker-centered supervisor usually attains higher productivity than one with a production-centered supervisor. However, individual circumstances are tremendously important. Much depends on the group's makeup; its expectancies; the ambitions, pay, and status of its members; and past experiences of members and the group. There are cases in which the production-centered supervisor obtains excellent results. But the evidence favors the worker-centered supervisor who believes it is the human element that ultimately controls productivity. Such a supervisor's attention is centered on the human aspects of work performance. The worker-centered supervisor creates a favorable supervisor-employee relationship based on mutual belief that team members, as human beings, will aspire to accomplish goals when appreciation is shown that their efforts are satisfactory and essential.

The supervisor's commitment to improved productivity is essential. A supervisor should be personally involved in figuring out ways to increase production. It must also be recognized that some causes of low-team productivity are beyond the jurisdiction of the supervisor. The five steps discussed below can help a supervisor improve team productivity.

1. Set an improvement goal and decide where to start. All available facts are used to determine the present performance level, which is then compared with what the supervisor and group members believe should be accomplished. Improvement is sought first in areas of high volume or where present operations appear to be poor. Mutual agreement on where to start is obtained. There should also be agreement on how the improvement will be determined, but the team should avoid getting bogged down in measurement schemes.

2. Remove obstacles standing in the way of improvement. When a list of obstacles believed to be retarding better production is created, a lengthy list is likely but it usually can be boiled down to the more common causes: wrong materials, machine breakdowns, bad maintenance, low quality of work, insufficient instructions, excess paperwork, poor physical working conditions, the operator's lack of freedom to make minor decisions. Full participation should be sought when seeking ways to remove or minimize these obstacles.

3. Make certain the sought-for improvements are thoroughly known to all team members and that members are committed to achieving them. An informed and dedicated team is needed to get the job done; everyone must know what is going to be done, and how. Point out to group members that high-production levels generate self-respect and personal satisfaction. The supervisor should be alert to undercurrents of discontent, should find out what's wrong, and should act immediately to correct problems.

4. Improve the effectiveness of the team's efforts. This factor emphasizes the importance of people in any undertaking. The abilities of each team member should be assessed, and if they are not adequate, that member should be given extra training or instruction or possibly transferred to work that is in keeping with the employee's skills.

5. Keep group members fully informed of progress. The members of a productive team want to know how they are doing. Information on how, when, and why production is proceeding has favorable effects because it tells them where the team stands and gives them recognition for what they are doing. Such information should be frequently given, along with reasons why actual production may be above or below expectancy.

Chapter 10

COUNSELING AND APPRAISING

Sooner or later almost every employee encounters a personal problem. Frequently the supervisor is asked for advice or to help solve the problem. Typically, the supervisor spends considerable time in providing such assistance. Many of these problems are work oriented or concerned with job duties, responsibilities, or personnel relationships. Others are not directly connected with work yet can have a real effect upon work performance. Such problems may pertain to the employee's family, financial affairs, or health.

IMPORTANCE OF COUNSELING

Supervisory counseling involves the willingness and the availability of supervisors to talk over personal problems with their employees. The mutual exchange of opinion on what might be done to alleviate a difficulty is generally beneficial. Of course, counseling is not restricted to supervisors and their subordinates. Much counseling takes place among supervisors and between supervisors and staff people. However, in most cases, supervisors must serve as counselors whether they choose to do so or not; employees are going to come to them with problems.

Counseling is important in supervision for two major reasons. First, it helps to identify problems affecting productivity and human relationships. Commonly, the viewpoint of another person is helpful in discovering causes and making it possible to see exactly what the difficulty is. Once the problem is known, effective steps can then be taken to correct it. The second reason counseling is important is that it helps to develop an environment of openness and trust. It is helpful for employees to know they are working for, or with, someone who is familiar with their work situation and who is experienced in solving personal problems.

BASICS OF COUNSELING

There are certain things that a supervisor can do to help when counseling employees. Some of these are discussed below.

1. Get the employee to talk freely. One way to achieve this is to talk about matter-of-fact subjects such as the employee's hobby, favorite sport, or family. Casual conversation that may reveal new insights into the employee's difficulties should be encouraged.

2. Be empathic and verify your understanding of the situation. The supervisor must recognize and try to understand the situation from the employee's point of view. There will be different views, but the one that should most condition what corrective action is to be taken, if any, is how the employee sees it. In addition, the supervisor must make certain the facts have been gathered. Summary statements such as "Now, is what you mean. . . ." or "It's your opinion that. . . ." can help clear up confusion both in the employee's mind and in the supervisor's understanding.

3. Don't hurry the interview. Good counseling requires time. If necessary, the interview can be continued at an additional session. Pauses may indicate that the employee is struggling to organize thoughts or to comprehend what was just said. It can be a mistake to try to fill up the entire time with conversation. The employee should also be permitted to disgress and to express ideas. Rambling thoughts might help the employee bypass a mental roadblock or hang-up. Careful listening can reveal important clues to the difficulty.

4. Permit employees to identify problems and develop their own solutions. The counselor's function is to help the employee help himself or herself. When such self-development takes place, the employee gains self-confidence and self-reliance. At the end of the counseling session, the employee should have the feeling that the problem is known, and the action to be taken should be clear and acceptable. It is usually helpful to have a follow-up meeting to resolve any difficulties that may arise and to check progress.

NONDIRECTIVE COUNSELING

The term, *nondirective counseling*, is used when employees diagnose their own problems, develop their own solutions, decide what actions they are going to take, and receive help from the supervisor by their request only. In this type of counseling, the supervisor acts like a mirror and merely reflects the employees' feelings and beliefs. Hopefully this helps employees to see themselves better and to realize the possibilities of the corrective actions that might be taken.

As indicated above, there should be considerable participation by the employee in all counseling. However, in nondirective counseling little direction is given by the supervisor, who takes the restricted yet vital role of being silent and listening. The supervisor asks a few skillful questions to reveal the details and the excuses or reasons that shed light on the employee's present feelings and beliefs. Figure 10–1 outlines the significant differences between directive counseling and nondirective counseling.

FIGURE 10–1
Selected characteristics of directive and nondirective counseling

Characteristics	Directive counseling	Nondirective counseling
Talking controlled by	Supervisor	Employee
Emphasis given to	Facts	Feelings
Subject selection by	Supervisor	Employee
Conclusion reached	Yes	No

PROS AND CONS OF THE SUPERVISOR AS COUNSELOR

Some things work to the advantage of a supervisor who counsels. For example, counseling sets up a relationship whereby employee behavior, wants, and dislikes can become known to the supervisor. Frequently this familiarity extends to off-work activities. In addition, the supervisor's contact with employees is usually continuous; the supervisor sees them daily or hourly or even more frequently. It is therefore possible to observe what is happening to the employees, to act quickly if needed, and to follow up closely on whatever actions are taken.

There are also disadvantages. The close relationship may lead employees to believe that the supervisor cannot be an objective counselor. They may see the supervisor as too much a part of the same environment, and therefore an outsider would be better—the old story of familiarity breeding contempt. The employee might well feel that the supervisor is not the proper person to talk with if a violation of a company rule is involved, since the supervisor represents formal authority. Some supervisors avoid counseling because they believe they lack the proper training and know-how. Supervisors who are inclined to think and act in terms of accomplishing work goals may consider counseling too time-consuming.

PERFORMANCE APPRAISAL

Appraising employee performance is one of the most difficult and yet important parts of the supervisor's job. All supervisors are constantly making decisions concerning the contributions and abilities of their employees. Some employees show more initiative than others; others have a great deal of ability but must be constantly pushed. Performance appraisal cannot be avoided, and it is wanted by employees. It is normal to want to know how one is doing. Is the work satisfactory? What can be done to gain a better rating?

The goal of employee appraisal is to improve results. Performance appraisal should be viewed as a necessary part of good supervision, not as a substitute for supervision. No system of appraisal will do what the supervisor cannot accomplish.

Specifically, performance appraisal aids in informing employees where they stand, in encouraging self-development, and in giving proper recognition to employees. A systematic, periodic assessment of each subordinate has the additional advantages of ensuring that high-potential workers are placed in challenging jobs and that underperformers are identified so they can be helped. Figure 10–2 outlines the potential benefits of performance appraisal.

Performance appraisals are handled in most organizations in one of two ways. Informal appraisals occur in all organizations. Many small businesses have informal appraisal systems. Under such a system no formal procedures, methods, or times are established for conducting performance appraisals. Under this type of system, the appraisal is conducted by the supervisor informally, giving the employee a general impression of how the supervisor feels about the employee's performance. Unfortunately, in all too many cases, the appraisal is conducted only when the employee has made a mistake. The employee often develops negative feelings about this type of performance appraisal.

The second approach to performance appraisals is to have a formalized appraisal system. Under a formal appraisal system, procedures, methods, and times are established for conducting performance appraisals.

FIGURE 10–2
Benefits of performance systems to the organization, the supervisor, and the employee

Benefits to the organization:
1. Provides an evaluation of the organization's human resources.
2. Gives a basis for making future personnel decisions.
3. Increases the potential of present personnel meeting the present and future needs of the organization.
4. Improves employee morale.

Benefits to the supervisor:
1. Provides a clearer picture of the employee's understanding of what is expected on the job.
2. Gives the supervisor input into each employee's development.
3. Improves productivity and morale of employees.
4. Helps identify capable replacements for higher level jobs within the supervisor's work unit.

Benefits to the employee:
1. Allows the employee to present ideas for improvement.
2. An opportunity to change the employee's behavior is provided.
3. Lets the employee know how the supervisor feels about job performance.
4. Assures the employee of regular and systematic reviews of performance.

It is important to note that formal appraisal systems also contain an informal element. For example, general comments made by a supervisor about an employee's performance are a form of informal performance appraisal. Supervisors must realize that any comment made by a supervisor about an employee's performance is viewed by the employee as a performance appraisal. Thus, the supervisor must use these informal reviews to reinforce good performance and discourage poor performance.

PERFORMANCE APPRAISAL METHODS

Ideally, performance appraisals should be directly related to job success. However, locating or creating satisfactory measures of job success can be difficult. There are many jobs that can't be objectively measured. For example, evaluating the performance of certain employees is extremely difficult. In addition, job performance is often influenced by factors outside the employee's control. For example, the performance of a machine operator is partially influenced by the age and condition of the equipment. For these reasons and others, performance appraisals are often based on personal characteristics and other subjective factors. Some of the personal characteristics that are frequently used in performance appraisal systems are integrity, dependability, attitude, initiative, judgment, and others.

Numerous problems exist in performance appraisal systems based on personal characteristics. Supervisors often resist this type of process. The major reason for their resistance is that this type of system places the supervisor in the position of being a judge, with the employee being the defendant. Another problem is the temptation of the supervisor to favor close friends and associates. Because it is natural to see favorable characteristics in friends, the supervisor may never realize that favoritism is interfering. Despite all these problems, performance appraisal systems based on personal characteristics and subjective evaluations are still in widespread use.

Some of the most frequently used performance appraisal methods are discussed below.

1. Rating scale. Under this method certain factors such as initiative, dependability, cooperativeness, quality of work, and so forth, are printed on a form and opposite each factor is a rating scale for evaluating the respective factor. The points or values assigned to each factor may or may not be included on the form, but a description should be included to help guide the rater. The points given for each factor are then added to determine the final score or rating.

2. Ranking. All persons are appraised by ranking in an array from top to bottom, showing the best, next best, and so forth.

3. Paired comparison. Each person is compared with every other person of the work group. Employee A is compared with B, C, D, and so forth. Then, employee B is compared with A, C, and D, and so forth. Performances are tallied, and the total score determines the ranking of each employee.

4. Forced choice. The rating form consists of many groups of five statements. For each group the rater marks the statement most descriptive and least descriptive of each employee. The statements are tallied, and the employee's total score is determined. Because the value associated with each statement is not known to the rater, it is claimed that this method has less bias than other methods.

5. Critical incidents. The supervisor records favorable as well as unfavorable critical incidents that reveal each employee's behavior and accomplishments. Such an approach helps the rater remember all significant happenings. A rating can then be determined by reviewing and consolidating the incidents.

6. Management by objectives (MBO). MBO, discussed in Chapter 3, is often used as a performance appraisal system. Under MBO the supervisor serves as an available resource to help the employee reach the goals that were mutually established by the employee and the supervisor. The employee's performance is then evaluated based on the degree to which the agreed-upon objectives were achieved.

TRAPS TO AVOID IN PERFORMANCE APPRAISAL

In determining employee appraisals, the supervisor should be careful to measure the employee's performance only on the current job and not on a previous job. It should also be remembered that the appraisal covers the entire period of the rating, and the rater should not concentrate on only the last two weeks or be unduly influenced by an incident that took place five months ago. The rater should also avoid emphasis on two or three favorite traits; all traits being appraised should be taken into consideration and given adequate thought in relationship to each employee. It is the overall viewpoint of performance that is important.

The "halo effect," whereby a high rating given one characteristic tends to result in a high rating for all factors, should be avoided. It is possible for an employee to rate high on one trait but quite low on others. An effective procedure is to rate all members on one trait, then all on the next trait, then on the third trait, and so forth. Another effect to be avoided is "central tendency," whereby every employee is given an average score on every trait. There are no extremes of very good or very poor. When this happens there is no appraisal, since no strengths or weaknesses are revealed, a condition most unlikely to exist in any sizable group. Central tendency indicates a need for training in rating methods and modifications in the means of appraisal being used.

THE APPRAISAL INTERVIEW

Merely evaluating the employee's performance is part of the supervisor's job in the performance appraisal process. The other part of the job is communicating the appraisal to the employee. The purposes of communicating the performance appraisal are to (1) provide the employee a clear understanding of how the supervisor feels the employee is performing, (2) clear up any misunderstandings about what is expected, (3) establish a program of improvement, and (4) improve the working relationship between the supervisor and the employee.

Effective performance appraisal interviews are the result of good planning by the supervisor. First, the supervisor should give considerable thought and time to the evaluation that is going to be given. Whatever form that the supervisor's organization uses for performance appraisals, considerable time and thought should be given to completing the form. The form should not be completed in the few minutes before the interview. When feasible the employee should be given a week's notice concerning the upcoming performance appraisal.

A private room or office should be used, interruptions should be held to a minimum, and the confidential nature of the information should be explained to the employee. The performance appraisal interview is not the time to tell the employee off. You are trying to make the job easier for the employee and to help the employee become happier and more productive. Figure 10–3 gives some questions that the supervisor should consider before discussing the performance appraisal with the employee.

Once the interview is under way, let the employee express his or

FIGURE 10–3
Questions that should be answered by the supervisor prior to the performance appraisal interview

1. What are the specific good points on which you will compliment the employee?
2. What are the specific bad points that you intend to discuss?
3. What reactions do you anticipate? How do you intend to handle these reactions?
4. Can you support your performance appraisal with adequate facts?
5. What specific help or corrective action do you anticipate offering?
6. What is your approach for gaining acceptance to your suggested corrective action?
7. What follow-up action do you have in mind?

her thoughts. Do not rush the interview or let it drag out and become a repetition of the same few issues. Give deserved praise but also forcefully point out those areas where improvement is needed. Together with the employee, develop a definite program for the employee to follow to improve.

SALARY RECOMMENDATIONS AND PERFORMANCE APPRAISALS

There is no consensus concerning how frequently performance appraisals should be conducted. The answer to this question is as frequently as is necessary in order to let the employees know how they are doing. Most organizations require a formal performance appraisal at least once a year. However, most employees want to know more frequently than once a year how well they are doing. Therefore, it is recommended that the supervisor do at least two or three informal reviews each year in addition to the formal performance appraisal.

Generally, it is undesirable to discuss salary recommendations during the formal performance appraisal interview. The primary reason for this is that it often places employees on the defensive and inhibits learning. Performance appraisals should be concerned with reviewing past performance and planning a program for future performance. If, during the entire evaluation, employees are thinking about what their raises are going to be, then generally little learning occurs. Salary increases should certainly be based on performance. However, annual salary review sessions should be held separately from the formal performance appraisal session. Usually salary reviews should be held two or three weeks after the formal performance review.

Chapter 11

HANDLING ABSENTEEISM AND TARDINESS

The problems of absenteeism and tardiness faced by supervisors appear to be inevitable. However, much can be done by supervisors to keep absence and tardy rates within reasonable bounds. This is desirable from the viewpoint of self-interest alone, because supervisors are affected by them more than anybody else. The absence of an employee, for example, may mean that a replacement must be found, a change in work assignment must be made, or a delay in getting certain work completed must be accepted. Costs increase when schedules are disrupted, machines are idled, or a wanted service is delayed.

Few realize the actual cost of absenteeism. Estimates range from 1 to 5 percent of total payroll costs. This means that the yearly output of over two million employees is lost. Furthermore, the indirect cost of absenteeism is believed to be three to four times greater than the direct cost. The problem appears to be increasing; absentee rates have shown a steady rise since the beginning of the 1960s.

Are absenteeism and tardiness facts of life that must be accepted? To a degree, the answer is yes. Employees have personal business to take care of, they get sick, they have accidents, and they have unpredictable experiences that keep them from their jobs. Absenteeism and tardiness for these reasons may be termed unavoidable. There is also another classification of absenteeism and tardiness—avoidable—in which the employee could come to work, and on time, but does not do so. It is this type of absenteeism and tardiness that the supervisor can influence.

FACTS ABOUT ABSENTEEISM

Often it is difficult to distinguish between unavoidable and avoidable absenteeism. However, experience has proven that absenteeism is not equally distributed among all employees. It has been found that 50 percent of absenteeism comes from only 5 to 10 percent of all employees. Furthermore, it has been found that approximately 50 percent of the work force will have perfect attendance. In general, the high absentee is more difficult to supervise, harder to get along with, and has few friends. Those employees who are adaptable to change, who are liked by others, and who are interested in their work tend to have low or no absenteeism. The following facts have also been discovered:

1. Absenteeism is likely to be higher on Mondays, Fridays, and the day before or following a holiday.
2. Distance traveled to work and weather do not appear to be related to absenteeism.
3. The absenteeism rate (in percentage) is higher in large companies than in small companies.
4. Despite higher health levels, absenteeism has increased during the past 15 years.
5. Absenteeism in offices is generally about one half as much as in factories.
6. Employees with high absenteeism rates their first year with a company will usually continue this pattern during following years.

All of the above suggest that the personality of the offender, the interactions among group members, the work, the environment, and the supervisor all influence the amount of absenteeism. The precise effect of these factors varies from situation to situation. In certain cases the personality, attitude, background, and beliefs of the employee are dominant, and no amount of trying to understand or censuring will alter the situation. It appears, however, that in most cases the problems, or what the employee believes are the problems, are aggravated by the job or the job relationships—job boredom or bad relationships with a supervisor or fellow employees. When these cause absenteeism, the supervisor can and should take action. Regardless of the type of work, the way employees are treated by the supervisor and other group members has a definite relationship to their absenteeism records. Further, the degree of job satisfaction employees derive from their work and the general working climate are related to absenteeism.

THE ROOT OF THE PROBLEM

The supervisor's first step in reducing absenteeism is to be sincerely concerned and to face up to the problem. The tendency of most supervisors is to lash out at the offender with a harsh warning. The trouble with this approach is that it addresses only the symptoms and not the cause of the problem. Also, any improvement realized will usually be short lived—perhaps a week or two.

A better approach is to individually analyze each absenteeism problem. When an employee is absent the supervisor should first check the employee's attendance record. If the record suggests a problem, the supervisor should talk about the problem when the employee returns. It should be kept in mind that there is a big difference between the person who has been absent for 12 days due to a foot operation and the person who has averaged missing two days a week for the past six weeks.

The problems and causes uncovered will be numerous. However, one of the more frequently encountered reasons is that the job is boring and offers little or no challenge to the employee. In this situation the employee often believes that the job holds no future. Another frequently expressed reason for absenteeism is that it seems to make little difference whether the employee is present or absent. The final product or service does not seem to be affected as far as the employee can see. In other instances there will be indications that the absentee does not get along with fellow group members and may stay away from the job to avoid personal problems. The employee who has not worked in some time may find it difficult to adapt to working five days a week. Also, there are employees who have watched the late-late TV show or partied so late that they could not get up in the morning.

WHAT CAN THE SUPERVISOR DO?

The identification of the cause of the absenteeism problem usually suggests what actions the supervisor needs to take. Precisely what measure can be taken will vary according to the particular needs of the individual organization. The following are some suggestions:

1. Screen out applicants who have a propensity to be absent. It may be best to avoid the problem by not hiring a person who is likely to be absent a great deal. The supervisor's experience and study of the applicant's behavior will prove helpful in determining this, but knowledge of such things as past attendance records, personal problems, and hours of work preference may also prove beneficial.

2. Have an attendance policy and make it known to every employee. It should be pointed out that the employees are expected to be regular in attendance, and its importance to the organization should be specified. Advance notice of absence when possible should be required. Notice should be given as far in advance as possible and should specify the reason for the proposed absence.

3. Instill in employees responsibility for the finished product or service. Supervisors should go out of their way to help employees understand how their personal efforts are needed. Special efforts should be made to communicate effectively the problems that arise when employees do not report for work.

4. Redesign jobs or transfer employees to other work. If dissatisfaction with the job itself appears to be the cause of absenteeism, consideration should be given to restructuring some of the tasks or activities in the department. The job may be repetitive, it may not use the employee's skills, or it may have little responsibility. The challenge for the supervisor is to determine if these conditions exist, and if so, what to do about them. The boredom in some jobs can be lessened through job enrichment (this was discussed in Chapter 7). Some employees want and seek responsibility; others do not. It is the supervisor's job to determine who does and who does not. Those desiring responsibility should be given it whenever possible. Those wishing to avoid responsibility should not be given any more than necessary. Another possibility includes employees who don't get along with their peers. When this occurs the supervisor should confront the problem directly and try to help resolve the differences. If this doesn't work, the supervisor may be forced to separate the employees.

5. Counsel employees. Supervisors must let employees know they are willing to help. One method that can be effective is to require all employees who have been absent to report to the supervisor before starting work. This provides supervisors with a natural opportunity to counsel employees. The purpose should be to help employees, to find out the real reasons for being off the job, and to ascertain whether situations causing absences can be brought under control.

6. Allow a certain amount of time for personal business. Too many times employees call in sick when actually time off is needed to conduct personal business. Honesty is promoted when employees know the supervisor is flexible on this matter and will try to accommodate them whenever possible. Advance notice must be insisted upon, however. When a good understanding exists between employees and supervisors, employees will usually show their appreciation by meeting work deadlines in spite of absences.

7. Keep up-to-date, accurate attendance records. Such information is the factual foundation for keeping absenteeism within reasonable limits. Individual records for each employee should reflect the overall picture of absences, their duration, time of absence notification, and a brief summary of discussions and interviews.

8. Use programmed attendance. In this relatively new approach, an absentee rate for the group is agreed to by the supervisor and the employees. This rate is made known to the employees, and they are allowed to divide up this time and administer the program. If one member takes excessive time, the matter is handled by the other members of the group. Advocates of this arrangement report considerable success with it.

9. Give rewards for excellent attendance. This practice, while used successfully by some companies, is frowned upon by others that have found it rewards the habitually good attenders but fails to reach absentee offenders. Rewards may be a pair of theater tickets, a set of dishes, and so forth. The success of such a program no doubt depends upon individual circumstances, with special emphasis on the supervisor's belief in, and enthusiasm for, this practice.

10. Distribute lost-time statistics. Regular distribution of such information will help impress employees with the importance of being on the job. It will also demonstrate the company's interest in minimizing absenteeism. The trend of absenteeism in the department can be shown, along with what areas are contributing the least and the most to the absenteeism level.

TARDINESS

Tardiness is of as much concern to the supervisor as absenteeism. When an employee does not appear for work on time, the process is held up and planned schedules cannot be followed. Tardiness stems from failure to realize the need and obligation to be on time. Usually tardy employees give little thought to the inconvenience and extra cost they cause their employers. Time either is not important to them, or they fail to allow themselves sufficient time to get ready for work. Unless corrected firmly but fairly, tardiness can become habitual.

In many instances the corrective action for tardiness follows the same lines as those indicated above for absenteeism. Like absenteeism, tardiness can be categorized as: (1) unavoidable or accidental and (2) avoidable or controllable. In the first category are absences that will occur no matter what the supervisor does; they may be due to a severe storm or an emergency at home. Avoidable absenteeism can and should be dealt with by the supervisor. To determine whether tardiness is unavoidable or avoidable, all tardiness should be noted.

In the case of controllable tardiness, the supervisor should identify consistent latecomers and try to ascertain the reasons for their tardiness. To do this, the supervisor should consult tardiness records and hold a private conference with each offender. During this conference the seriousness of the situation should be discussed and a plan for eliminating the problem should be agreed upon. Without making threats, the supervisor should make sure that the employee understands that the employee is expected to honor the agreed-upon plan. The supervisor should then follow up closely to see that the problem diminishes. If the tardiness persists, talk to the employee again and emphasize that the tardiness must stop or disciplinary action will be taken. If the tardiness continues, follow the formal disciplinary procedure and discipline the employee. (Discipline is discussed in depth in Chapter 16.)

Some useful information regarding tardiness is as follows:

1. The more employees feel needed on the job, the more likely it is that they will be there on time.
2. A favorable supervisor-member relationship helps to keep tardiness at a low level.
3. A relatively small group of chronic offenders usually accounts for the majority of tardiness. Apparently, being on time is in part a matter of self-discipline.
4. Older employees, both in service and age, tend to be on time more than younger employees.

Chapter 12

HANDLING CONFLICT

Conflict is inevitable in organizations. As such, the supervisor is routinely faced with conflict situations and must learn how to effectively deal with these situations. Unfortunately, too many supervisors view conflict as something that should be avoided at all costs. Conflict can have positive as well as negative effects. Effective supervisors learn to curb the negative effects of conflict and to guide the conflict toward positive results.

THE EFFECTS OF CONFLICT

The negative aspects of conflict are generally quite obvious. Some of the potential negative effects are that the work of the organization may suffer. For example, most people can think of conflict situations in their organization that have diverted time, energy, and money away from the organization's goals. Furthermore, it is entirely possible for a conflict to become continuous and cause additional harm to the organization. It is possible that the conflict may cause one or more employees to leave the organization. Conflict can adversely affect the health of the involved parties. Intense conflict can also lead to behaviors such as sabotage, stealing, lying, distortion of information, and other similar actions that can have negative effects on the organization.

On the other hand, when it is properly managed, conflict can have some very useful benefits. Some of these are listed below:

1. Conflict usually causes changes. In attempting to determine the cause of the conflict and in developing a solution to the conflict, changes occur.
2. Conflict activates people. It helps to eliminate monotony and boredom in that it wakes people up and gets them moving.
3. Conflict is a form of communication. Recognizing the conflict may open up new and more effective channels of communication.

4. Conflict can be healthy in that it relieves pent-up emotions and feelings.
5. Conflict can be educational in that the participants in a conflict situation can and often do not only learn a great deal about themselves but also about the other people involved.
6. The aftermath of conflict can produce a stronger and better work environment.

THE STAGES OF CONFLICT

Conflict is a dynamic process that does not usually appear suddenly. In fact, conflict generally passes through several stages:

1. Latent conflict—At this stage, the basic conditions for conflict exist but have not been recognized by the involved parties.
2. Perceived conflict—The basic conditions for conflict are recognized by one or both of the parties.
3. Felt conflict—Internal tensions begin to build in the involved parties, but the conflict is still not out in the open.
4. Manifest conflict—The conflict is out in the open and the existence of the conflict becomes obvious to other parties who are not involved.
5. Conflict aftermath—The conflict is stopped by some method. How the conflict is stopped establishes new conditions that lead either to a new conflict or to more effective cooperation between the involved parties.

A particular conflict situation does not necessarily pass through all of the stages. In addition, the parties who are involved in the conflict may not be at the same stage at the same time. For example, it is entirely possible for one party to be at the manifest stage and one party be at the perceived stage.

TYPES OF CONFLICT IN ORGANIZATIONS

Conflict can occur either internal to an individual or external to an individual. Conflict that is internal to an individual is called intrapersonal conflict. Conflict that is external to an individual falls into three general types—interpersonal, structural, and strategic.

Intrapersonal conflict. Because intrapersonal conflict is internal to individuals, it is very difficult to analyze. Intrapersonal conflict can result when barriers exist between individuals' drives or motives and the achieving of their goals. For example, female or black employees who feel that they have not received a promotion because of their race or sex are very likely to experience intrapersonal conflict. This situation often leads to frustration on the part of these individuals. Intrapersonal conflict can also occur when goals have both positive and negative aspects and when competing or conflicting goals exist. Figure 12–1 shows how intrapersonal conflict can occur.

Interpersonal conflict.   Interpersonal conflict is external to the individual and can result from many factors. Interpersonal conflict can occur between two supervisors, between two of a supervisor's employees, between the supervisor and the boss, or between a supervisor and one of the supervisor's employees.

One cause of interpersonal conflict is opposing personalities. Some people just seem to rub each other the wrong way. An example of this might be a person who is constantly playing practical jokes and a person who is quiet and reserved. These two people, if they are in regular contact with each other, might experience interpersonal conflict because of their differing personalities.

Prejudices based on personal background or other origins also can cause interpersonal conflict. Everyone is familiar with the potential that exists for conflict based on racial, sexual, or religious differences. Other, more subtle prejudices can also cause interpersonal conflict. Possible examples include the college graduate versus the person without a college degree, the married person versus the divorced person, and the experienced employee versus one who has just been hired.

Jealousy and envy also are sources of interpersonal conflict. Supervi-

FIGURE 12–1
Sources of intrapersonal conflict

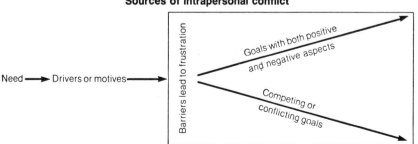

sors sometimes experience this form of conflict when they are first promoted. Prior to the promotion, the supervisor was one of the gang. However, after the promotion, conflict can develop, due partially to envy and jealousy, between former peers and the supervisor.

Structural conflict. Structural conflict results from the nature of the organizational structure. Structural conflict is independent of the personalities involved. For example, the marketing department naturally wants the production department to produce every size and color that the customer could possibly imagine. The production department, of course, wants to limit the number of sizes and colors of the product. This type of conflict is just a natural by-product of the organizational structure and outlook of the various departments.

Strategic conflict. Intrapersonal, interpersonal, and structural conflicts are usually not planned by the people who are involved. They generally just happen, due to the circumstances. On the other hand, strategic conflicts are planned and often intentionally started. Generally, this type of conflict results from the promotion of self-interest on the part of an individual or group. The individual or group that starts the conflict intends to get an advantage over the other party. For example, when a new project is going to be started and is viewed as being very worthwhile, managers within the organization often engage in strategic conflict to gain control of the project.

Strategic conflicts do not necessarily mean that the participants are unethical or dishonest. The reward structure of many organizations often encourages strategic conflicts. If this type of conflict is managed properly, it can have the positive effects that were described earlier in this chapter. Unfortunately, this type of conflict can easily become unfair and result in severe negative outcomes.

MANAGING CONFLICT

Supervisors most frequently deal with intrapersonal and interpersonal conflict. As was stated earlier, intrapersonal conflict is the most difficult to analyze. Supervisors should not go around looking for intrapersonal conflict in every situation. However, when an employee asks to discuss a personal problem with the supervisor, the supervisor should look for signs of intrapersonal conflict. At the same time, the supervisor should be very cautious in giving advice relating to intrapersonal problems. In fact, the supervisor should normally refer the employee to a person who is more qualified (pastor or psychologist) to handle the problem. If the intrapersonal conflict develops to the point where it is affecting the employee's work performance, then the supervisor must take action.

Chapter 13

SUPERVISING MINORITY GROUPS

The U.S. work force of today is heterogeneous, including male and female members from various ethnic, racial, and religious backgrounds. It is difficult to identify a majority group, but common usage refers to certain racial, handicapped, or age groups as minority groups. In addition, women employees are usually considered a minority group, although in recent years over 40 percent of the full-time work force and two thirds of the part-time workers in this country have been female.

Historically, minority groups have suffered varying degrees of discrimination in the areas of hiring, job assignments, wages, performance evaluations, promotions, layoffs, recalls, discipline, and discharges. While legislation has been passed to prohibit discrimination, it is often up to the supervisor to implement these laws and to see that discrimination does not occur.

MINORITY GROUPS

When most people hear the term *minority group* they immediately think of women or blacks. Although women and blacks constitute the two largest minority groups, they are by no means the only groups. Older employees, the physically or mentally handicapped, and other ethnic and racial groups make up some other frequently encountered minority groups. It should always be kept in mind that minority group members have basically the same needs and wants as any other workers.

Women. As of 1980, almost 50 percent of the work force was composed of women. This represents an increase from less than 20 percent in 1900.

It should be recognized that the principal reason women work is not to pass the time or for self-fulfillment. Women today work primarily because of economic need—to support themselves or others. Although their degree of participation in some fields is small, women have been employed in almost every occupational area: as executives, supervisors, accountants, machine operators, police officers, mail carriers, umpires, jockeys, and taxicab drivers. Women today are increasingly seeking and being given equal opportunities for employment and advancement.

A comparison of male and female employment in the United States shows, however, two outstanding discrepancies. First, there is an appreciable gap in earnings between males and females. Second, there is evidence that the knowledge and skills of working women are not being fully utilized. In other words, males are still getting most of the really good jobs.

Racial minorities. Like other minority groups, employees who are members of racial minorities want a fair chance to be part of the mainstream of action, to keep or advance in their jobs, and to enjoy life. While some may not have the qualifications considered desirable for certain types of work, due to lack of education or opportunity, they usually have a strong desire to make good and will seek help to make themselves better employees. If given the opportunity, they are as likely to measure up to performance standards as are other employees.

By far the best supervisory policy to follow is to forget any racial differences and treat all employees alike. For the supervisor to adopt special attitudes toward employees anticipates certain problems that seldom occur. Any special measures may also tend to perpetuate differences among employees.

Older employees. Older employees usually are thought of as those over 55 years of age. At about this time, changes due to aging normally begin to slowly take place. These changes vary in individuals and may or may not affect performance. In any case, decisions made regarding any employee should be based on the ability to do a job and not on the employee's age.

Most older employees gain a great deal of satisfaction from their work. It is likely to be the center of their interest and effort, and they recognize that through their work many of their needs will be satisfied. The supervisor should utilize older employees' cumulative experiences by asking them to share their knowledge with other employees, seeking their opinions, and pointing out their achievements to others. Such help from the supervisor can counter the tendencies of some older employees to become set in their ways.

Handicapped employees. The term *handicapped* is used here to refer to employees who have varying degrees of ability despite physical losses or mental disabilities. Handicapped employees are not totally disabled, and their productivity is frequently above average. Making jobs available to the handicapped is good business not only because they make good employees but also because having a job can provide them with a sense of belonging and acceptance by society.

There are numerous examples that demonstrate that handicapped persons can fill various types of jobs successfully. Like other minority group members, many handicapped workers will prove their ability if given a chance. They want to be a part of society, and they adjust well to others.

LAWS AFFECTING MINORITIES

In the United States considerable legislation has been enacted to provide equal opportunities in employment and pay and to prevent discrimination against any employee. The number of employees and the amount of business the organization does with the federal government determine which of these laws affect the organization. The following paragraphs provide a brief description of the most important laws affecting minority groups.

Title VII. Title VII of the Civil Rights Act of 1964, as amended by the Equal Employment Opportunity Act of 1972, has been the source for the greatest number of complaints concerning discrimination. The law prohibits discrimination based on race, color, religion, sex, or national origin in any term, condition, or privilege of employment. This law applies to all private employers of 15 or more people, all public and private educational institutions, all state and local governments, all public and private employment agencies, labor unions with 15 or more members, and joint labor-management committees for apprenticeships and training. This law established and gave the Equal Employment Opportunity Commission the power (1) to investigate job discrimination complaints, (2) to mediate an agreement between the parties to eliminate discrimination when the complaint is found to be justified, and (3) to take court action to enforce the law when necessary.

Title VI. Title VI of the 1964 Civil Rights Act prohibits discrimination based on race, color, or national origin in all programs or activities that receive federal financial aid in order to provide employment. Although this law does not prohibit sex discrimination, some federal agencies prohibit sex discrimination by their own regulations.

Equal Pay Act. The Equal Pay Act was passed in 1963 and was later amended by Title IX of the Education Amendments Act of 1972. The law requires all employers covered by the Fair Labor Standards Act (and others included in the 1972 extension) to provide equal pay to men and women who perform work that is similar in skill, effort, and responsibility. Title VII of the Civil Rights Act also requires equal pay regardless of race, national origin, or sex. This includes base pay as well as opportunities for overtime, raises, bonuses, commissions, and other benefits. The employer is also responsible for ensuring that all fringe benefits are equally available to all employees. Offering and paying higher wages to women and minorities in order to attract these groups is also illegal.

Education Amendments Act. Title IX of the Education Amendments Act of 1972 extended coverage of the Equal Pay Act of 1963. Title IX prohibits discrimination because of sex against employees or students of any educational institution receiving financial aid from the federal government.

Age Discrimination in Employment Act. The Age Discrimination in Employment Act was enacted in 1967 and amended in 1978. The act prohibits discrimination against people between the ages of 40 and 70 in any area of employment. This law applies to employers of 25 or more people. The law prohibits using age as a factor for making employment decisions.

Rehabilitation Act of 1973. The Rehabilitation Act of 1973, which was amended in 1977, prohibits employers from denying jobs to individuals merely because of a handicap. This law applies to government contractors and subcontractors with contracts of $50,000 or more and 50 or more employees. The act requires contractors to make reasonable and necessary accommodations to enable qualified handicapped people to work as effectively as other employees. This law defines a handicapped person as one who has a physical or mental impairment that significantly limits one or more major life activities.

Executive Order 11246—Executive Order 11375 (affirmative action). Executive Order 11246 was issued in 1965 and was amended by Executive Order 11375 in 1967. The order requires federal contractors and subcontractors to have affirmative action programs. The purpose of affirmative action programs is to increase employment opportunities for women and minorities in all areas of employment. The order further requires that employers with contracts or subcontracts over $50,000 and 50 or more employees develop and implement written affirmative action programs. These programs are monitored by the Office of Federal Contract Compliance (OFCC) of the United States Department of Labor.

ENFORCEMENT AGENCIES

There are two major federal enforcement agencies for equal employment opportunity. These are the Equal Employment Opportunity Commission (EEOC) and the Office of Federal Contract Compliance (OFCC). In the past, enforcement activities were conducted by many agencies. The trend has been toward consolidation of enforcement activities. It is probable that more consolidation will occur in the future, possibly forming one enforcement agency.

Affirmative action programs. Of all the requirements concerned with discrimination, affirmative action programs are by far the most controversial. Affirmative action programs are required of certain federal contractors and subcontractors and also may be required of employers who have been found guilty of certain discriminatory practices. Some employers and individuals mistakenly refer to equal employment opportunity as affirmative action. The elimination of hiring practices that have an adverse impact on minority groups is not affirmative action. Affirmative action refers to an employer's attempt to balance its work force in all job categories with respect to sex and race in order to reflect the same proportions as its general labor market. The employer prepares a plan with goals and timetables for the achievement of a balanced representation. When minorities and women have achieved employment and occupational parity in an organization, affirmative action programs are no longer necessary.

In recent years affirmative action has resulted in some reverse discrimination charges that have caused much confusion. The Supreme Court has ruled that discriminatory preference for any group, minority or majority, is illegal under the Civil Rights Act of 1964. The general interpretation is that preferential treatment of any person simply because he or she is a member of a minority group or was discriminated against in the past is forbidden.

Affirmative action programs that result in preferential treatment of certain groups also provoke resentment among employees. It is generally agreed that employers that are required to have affirmative action programs must make special efforts to increase the number of minorities and women in the work force but without discriminating against others.

Quotas for hiring minorities and women are not required by law. However, written goals are required under affirmative action guidelines. Opponents of affirmative action programs feel that written numerical goals, as in the case of quotas, force inflexible, unreasonable demands on employers. Opponents further argue that these goals result in the employer's striving for a numerical result rather than the primary goal of equal opportunity. Proponents of affirmative action, however, argue that written affirmative action goals are no different from any organizational goals where quantitative measures are applied. Only when an employer consistently fails to obtain its goals or when there is evidence that the employer has not acted in good faith will the enforcement agency step in to impose goals. By striving to eliminate discrimination within the organization, management can usually avoid court action and costly penalties.

A POSITIVE APPROACH TO EQUAL EMPLOYMENT OPPORTUNITY AND AFFIRMATIVE ACTION

Most people realize that there are many people who have not been utilized or have been underutilized in the past. The opportunity now exists for these people to be more fully employed. At the same time, opportunity exists for organizations to benefit from this new reservoir of talent. In all of the minority groups there are people who are not capable of doing the job. However, equal employment laws and affirmative action do not require employers to hire unqualified persons. In fact, establishing and using job-related factors for employment decisions allow only the most qualified to be employed and to advance within the organization. This means that all persons hired and advanced should be the most capable of performing the job.

Not only will equal employment opportunity benefit the organization, but it will benefit society as well. Past discrimination has resulted in segments of society being unable to find employment, especially meaningful employment. Research shows that these people are more likely to resort to welfare and crime than those who are meaningfully employed.

Management of today's organizations must provide positive leadership in the goal of equal employment opportunity just as it provides positive leadership in obtaining all other goals. Supervisors have a major impact on the implementation and achievement of this goal. It is necessary for supervisors to be fully aware of EEO and affirmative action goals. Supervisors must communicate these goals in a positive way to their subordinates. As with any organizational goal, the supervisor's attitude is important to the achievement of the goal. A negative or passive attitude will most likely result in problems for the supervisor and the organization. Figure 13–1 gives some suggestions that should help the supervisor in creating a positive atmosphere.

FIGURE 13–1
Suggestions for creating a positive EEO environment

1. Be aware of the legal and regulatory requirements of EEO and affirmative action that affect your organization.
2. Be aware of your organization's policies and practices that have resulted from EEO and affirmative action regulation.
3. Learn to recognize and eliminate stereotyping and preconceptions in expectations of women and minorities.
4. Provide clear, challenging, and achievable expectations for *all* of your subordinates.
5. Provide training, support, and encouragement that fit individual needs.
6. Be aware of and sensitive to issues that commonly arise in work forces comprised of different groups.
7. Help to facilitate the socialization of new employees.
8. Communicate with your employees to minimize isolation and maximize the contribution of all employees.
9. Provide adequate feedback on performance for all employees.
10. Avoid the extremes of "overprotection" and "abandonment" in dealing with minority group members.

Source: Adapted from Daniel H. Reigle, "Some Aspects of the Supervisor's Role in Affirmative Action," *Personnel Journal,* November 1978, pp. 606–8.

Chapter 14

SUPERVISING EMPLOYEES WITH SPECIAL PROBLEMS

Supervisors face a wide range of situations that involve employees' problems that must be handled and corrected if possible. A criterion in judging whether to handle personal problems is whether the behavior is unfavorably affecting the work output or the conditions under which the work is performed.

As discussed in Chapter 10, all employees have personal problems from time to time. Health problems, family problems, legal problems, and financial problems are some of the more common factors that influence performance on the job. These problems are normally solved privately by the individual or with a minimum of counseling and encouragement from the supervisor or someone else. There are some employees, however, who have lasting or recurring personal problems that are much more difficult to solve.

THE PROBLEM EMPLOYEE

Everyone lives in a stressful world. However, some people have more stress in their lives than others. In addition, some people have more trouble handling stress than others. Some work environments contribute to employee stress. Unfortunately, there is no known way for an organization to completely eliminate stress from the work place. Similarly, there is no way to completely eliminate stress from an employee's personal life. Stress seems to be an inherent part of each segment of our lives. Many people react to stress positively. However, some people need help in overcoming the personal problems that can result from stress.

There are many personal problems that may affect an employee's ability to work. Some employees are able to keep their personal lives separate from their work. They may be fully productive members of the work force and at the same time manage severe personal problems. Most employees are not like this. Most employees with severe personal problems cannot keep them from affecting their job performance. When an employee's job performance is affected by personal problems that cannot be corrected with normal counseling or disciplinary mea- sures, the employee is usually diagnosed as a problem employee.

There are many causes of severe personal problems. The problems already mentioned (health, family, legal, and financial) may be serious enough to cause the employee severe employment problems. Chronic diseases such as alcoholism, mental illness, drug dependency, and physi- cal illnesses are some of the common causes that create problem employ- ees. Severe family problems can also lead to mental problems that can in turn bring on drug dependence, illness, financial, and legal problems.

HOW THE PROBLEM EMPLOYEE AFFECTS
THE ORGANIZATION

The problem employee affects productivity and the work environ- ment in many ways. A primary result of personal problems brought to the work place is reduced productivity. Absenteeism and tardiness tend to increase. Another effect on productivity is reduced efficiency. Increased costs of insurance programs, including sickness and accident benefits, are a direct result of personal problems brought to the work place. Some industrial theft is due to the need for drug addicts to support their habits. Lower morale, more friction among employees, more friction between supervisors and employees, and more grievances also result from problem employees. Severe personal problems can sig- nificantly shorten the productive life of trained employees. Difficult to measure, but a very very real cost associated with problem employees is the loss of business and damaged public image.

In a 1977 Joint Report to Congress, the National Institute on Alco- hol Abuse and Alcoholism (NIAAA) and the Harvard School of Public Health estimated that alcoholism alone costs industry at least $15 billion dollars annually in terms of impaired job performance. The National Council on Alcoholism places the estimate at $25 billion dollars a year. The National Association for Mental Health estimated that in 1974 mental illness cost the United States nearly $20 billion dollars annually. Although few studies have estimated the cost of other employee problems to organizations, it is easy to see that the total cost is very large.

In addition to organizational cost, there are also costs to personal lives and society. Studies have shown that alcohol abuse is related to increased suicide, homicide, accidents, and diseases such as heart disease and cirrhosis. The total cost to the families affected by these problems may never be known. The human benefits from organizational attempts to solve these problems is a service to both the organization and society in general.

EMPLOYEE ASSISTANCE PROGRAMS (EAP)

Many large organizations and a growing number of smaller organizations are attempting to help the problem employee. This help is not purely altruistic but is based in large part on cost savings. These employee programs are generally referred to as employee assistance programs (EAP).

Until recent years, organizations attempted to avoid the employee's nonjob related problems. Although organizations were aware of the existence of these problems, they did not believe that the organization should interfere with the employee's personal life. In 1977, the previously described NIAAA and Harvard joint report was made public. This report showed the staggering cost of alcoholism and was instrumental in the development of employee assistance programs. At the same time, programs dealing with other nonjob related problems began developing.

There are several types of employee assistance programs. One type provides for diagnosis and treatment of the problem by the organization. The most common type of program employs a coordinator who sufficiently evaluates the employee's problem just to the degree that a proper referral to the appropriate agency or clinic can be made. Sometimes the coordinator is not a full-time employee of the organization but rather serves as a consultant.

DETECTING THE PROBLEM EMPLOYEE

As has been stated, it is not the supervisor's job to be concerned with an employee's personal problems unless work performance is affected. On the other hand, if an employee is having difficulties at work, the supervisor must not look the other way or cover up the difficulties because the employee has severe personal problems. In the past, supervisors, along with family and friends, have often attempted to help the employee avoid detection. Rationalizing that the problem or the reasons for the problems will go away only prolongs treatment for the problem employee. Overlooking rule violations and reduced productivity because the employee has personal problems may in fact be the worst thing a supervisor can do for both the employee and the organization.

The supervisor must learn how to detect evidence of deteriorating job performance. By properly documenting employee performance, the supervisor is able to detect a deterioration in an employee's performance. The supervisor should record evidence of deteriorating relationships, nonacceptable performance, and inability to follow rules.

The supervisor must be careful to be consistent in documenting performance problems. Noting inadequacies for one employee and not for others, just because the supervisor suspects the employee has a serious personal problem, is unfair. The supervisor should also consistently handle the evidence of poor performance for each employee. Overlooking examples of poor performance because the employee gives a particularly sad or convincing excuse may only prolong the problem. Figure 14–1 provides a checklist to aid in detecting a problem employee.

FIGURE 14–1
Detecting the problem employee

1. Be alert to, and document, changes in personality that affect working relationships.
   a. Insubordination.
   b. Altercations with other employees or with the supervisor.
2. Be alert to, and document, changes in quality and quantity of work.
   a. Reduced output.
   b. Increased errors or defects.
3. Be alert to, and document, rule violations.
   a. Unexcused absences.
   b. Unexcused tardiness.
   c. Leaving work station without permission.
   d. Dress code violations.
   e. Safety rules violations.
   f. Concealing or consuming drugs on company premises.
   g. Involvement with law, garnishment of wages, drug traffic.
4. Be consistent.

CONFRONTING THE PROBLEM EMPLOYEE

Once a problem employee has been identified, the supervisor must confront the employee. Most supervisors do not relish this responsibility. Sufficient documentation can greatly help the supervisor in this process. The confrontation between the supervisor and the problem employee should consist primarily of three steps: (1) performance criticism, (2) referral to the EAP, and (3) discussion of the consequences of the employee's actions.

The supervisor should first confront the employee with specific performance criticism. Reviewing any available documentation with the employee is a good approach. It helps the employee to realize that there is documented evidence of poor performance.

The supervisor should restrict criticism and discussion to job performance. Moralizing on the effects of drug abuse or other illnesses is not the supervisor's job. If the employee begins to talk about the problem, the supervisor should listen. However, it is not necessary to promote more discussion. Advising the employee should be limited to seeking help from the proper facilities.

The second part of the confrontation session is to refer the problem employee to counseling and assistance. At this point, the employee may become defensive or hostile. The supervisor should not be influenced by excuses or stories by the employee. Employees who have severe personal problems have had plenty of practice convincing themselves and others that their problems are caused by external forces beyond their control.

During this second part of the confrontation, the supervisor should emphasize that acceptance of assistance will not jeopardize the employee's job. In fact, it may be the only way the employee can continue to be employed by the organization. The supervisor should also emphasize that all aspects of the assistance program, including the discussion between the supervisor and the employee, are confidential. Some organizations do not even record the assistance in the employee's personnel file.

In this phase of the confrontation session, the supervisor should also discuss the need for performance improvement. If the employee accepts help, then most organizations agree to work with the employee on a schedule of improvement. If help is refused, the employee should be informed of the consequences. Usually if the employee does not accept assistance and the work performance does not improve, the

FIGURE 14–2
Confronting the problem employee

1. Phase one—performance criticism.
   a. Review documentation with employee.
   b. Restrict criticism to job performance.
   c. Do not diagnose the cause of the poor performance.
   d. Do not attempt to counsel on nature of problem.
2. Phase two—referral to counseling and assistance.
   a. Be firm and supportive.
   b. Be prepared for excuses and hostility.
   c. Explain that seeking help will not jeopardize job.
   d. Emphasize confidentiality of program.
   e. Know and discuss insurance coverage or other financial assistance.
3. Phase three—Discussion of consequences of employee action.
   a. Discuss need for improvement.
   b. Discuss possible consequences of not accepting help.
   c. Discuss success of program or similar programs.

employee is subject to discharge. The employee should also be informed that any improvement must be maintained in order to avoid discipline and discharge.

It is helpful at this point for the supervisor to discuss in general terms the success of the EAP or similar programs in other organizations. Once the employee realizes that the supervisor is aware of the poor performance, that something has to be done to correct it, and that there is a good chance of success, the employee is much more likely to cooperate. Figure 14–2 outlines the necessary steps in the confrontation between the supervisor and the problem employee.

AIDING AND EVALUATING RECOVERY

Once referral has been made to the assistance program, the employee is expected to become rehabilitated. The supervisor again bears the primary responsibility for evaluating rehabilitation. Evaluating the success of rehabilitation must be based on job performance. Other criteria such as abstinence for drug and alcohol abusers, certification of recovery by the assisting agency, or continued participation in the EAP are not as meaningful to the organization as improved job performance. The overriding objective of the supervisor and the organization should be that the employee not only recovers but also begins to function satisfactorily on the job.

When a supervisor has an employee who is participating in an assistance program, the supervisor can aid in the rehabilitation process by observing certain rules. First, the supervisor should continue to document the employee's job performance. Both problems and improvements should be noted. Second, the supervisor should ensure that the employee realizes that evidence of less than serious participation in the EAP will subject the employee to the discipline process. Third, the supervisor should follow EAP guidelines for rehabilitation expectations. The employee cannot be expected to recover overnight. The supervisor should be aware of organizational expectations for recovering employees. Fourth, the supervisor should not ignore problems just because the employee is in the EAP. Corrective discipline should be applied when the recovering employee does not perform up to expectations. Fifth, the supervisor should be watchful for improvement by the employee. Encouraging the continuation of the improvement by praise and other positive reinforcement is very helpful to the recovering employee. Sixth, the supervisor must preserve the confidentiality of the employee's personal problems and assistance. During the period of assistance, the supervisor may become aware of the specific problems affecting the employee. Sharing information of this type, even with higher management, is unethical and could subject the supervisor to legal action. The supervisor should, of course, inform upper management of the employee's participation in the EAP. The details of the particular problem are unnecessary for anyone other than the professionals with which the employee is dealing. Seventh, the supervisor should never dispense over-the-counter drugs such as cough medicine or aspirin to recovering employees. It is usually not wise for a supervisor to administer drugs of any kind to an employee. The primary reason for this is that even over-the-counter drugs may have negative side effects. This rule is of utmost importance for employees recovering from alcohol or drug dependency. Many over-the-counter drugs contain alcohol that can, even in small amounts, turn an alcoholic's recovery process around. In addition, some addictions, including alcohol, are sometimes treated with other drugs. These drugs can react violently with nonprescription drugs containing alcohol.

Chapter 15

LIVING WITH THE LABOR CONTRACT

Approximately 20 million employees in the United States are represented by labor unions. In unionized organizations, the supervisor is the primary link between the organization and the union members. The supervisor's first responsibility is to uphold the interests of management. At the same time, the supervisor must fulfill the contractual obligations of management and see that the union fulfills its obligations.

To understand the labor contract and how to live with it, the supervisor needs to know what actions of management and of labor are valid under collective bargaining, what practices have been designated unfair, and how to handle grievances.

THE SUPERVISOR'S RESPONSIBILITY TO THE EMPLOYER AND THE UNION

In a unionized organization the supervisor has a dual responsibility. The supervisor's first responsibility is, of course, to the employer. As a member of the management team, the supervisor must work toward achieving good productivity. As a member of management, the supervisor must also help to uphold the management commitments under the contract. The organization is held responsible by the union for any actions or lack of action by the supervisor in dealing with the union and its members. The Labor-Management Relations Act, passed in 1947, outlines some unfair labor practices that affect the supervisor. These include (1) restraining employees from forming or joining a union, (2) trying to influence a labor organization, (3) discriminating against union members, and, (4) discriminating against an employee for participating in a charge against the employer under the Labor-Management Relations Act.

A union can be either friendly or antagonistic toward management.

This friend-or-foe relationship is partially determined by how well supervisors do their jobs. The supervisors' relationship with the union begins during the union organization drive and continues during the negotiation and administration of the contract. Supervisors must know their responsibilities in these phases of the union relationship.

THE LABOR CONTRACT

Employers are required by law to bargain collectively with employees through representatives of the employees' choice. The National Labor Relations Board, upon request, conducts union representation elections.

If a union begins an organization drive, the supervisor is in an extremely precarious situation. In this situation the supervisor's actions are restricted by law. Strict adherence to the law is most important. Both the union and management can speak their minds about the other side. However, both parties are forbidden to use threats or reprisals or promises of benefits in order to get the employee to choose or not to choose union representation.

If a union is successful in becoming the representative of the employees, the supervisor must accept the situation. The supervisor must then learn to lead within the restraints set by the union. If the union and the organization develop a good relationship, there is much more flexibility within the restraints set by the union.

The specific contents of labor contracts vary. Most include the following subject areas, but the details are subject to wide variation:

1. The rights of management (not subject to bargaining).
2. The rights of unions to represent certain groups of employees.
3. Rates and levels of pay.
4. Hours and work schedules.
5. General working conditions.
6. Procedures for handling grievances.
7. Provision for reopening of clauses for subsequent bargaining.
8. Prohibition of discrimination for joining a union.
9. Employee discharge for just cause or for repeated performance failures.

The labor contract, when signed by both parties (the employer and the union representing the employees), sets the prescribed and agreed-to conditions under which the employer, the employees, and the union will work together. Disagreements are settled by use of a grievance procedure stated in the contract. (The grievance procedure is discussed in depth in a later section of this chapter.) If this proves ineffective in a given grievance, an outside third party (usually an arbitrator) may be called in to decide the issue.

THE UNION STEWARD

The union steward is both an employee of the organization and a union official. The union steward is elected by the union members. It is the steward who is the union's watchdog. The steward must be constantly aware of how the supervisor is administering the contract. It is often the steward who initiates a grievance. At the same time, however, it is to the supervisor's advantage to develop a good relationship with the steward. The relationship between the supervisor and the steward may be made even more difficult by the fact that the steward may work for the supervisor in performing normal work duties. However, showing respect for the steward's position is foremost in developing a good relationship. The following suggestions should help to foster a good relationship with the steward.

1. Keep the steward informed. A supervisor who tries to sneak changes through without the steward's knowledge is likely to have a grievance filed. It is much wiser for the supervisor to inform the steward and avoid unnecessary time-consuming grievances. Many times the steward can help to work out the little problems before they develop into grievances.

2. Show that you understand and appreciate the difficulty of the steward's job. The steward must serve two leaders: management as a good employee and the union as a good union official. The supervisor should not be more lenient with the steward than with the other employees. But, it helps to show consideration for the steward's position.

3. Show the steward a willingness to compromise. Supervisors must, of course, know when to compromise. They must be careful to compromise only on issues within their authority. For instance, a supervisor might agree not to discipline an employee for tardiness because of problems beyond the employee's control. Supervisors, however, should not agree to consult the union before using discipline for tardiness. Furthermore, supervisors must get their bosses' permission before making any exceptions to the contract.

GRIEVANCES

Employees have not always had the right to complain, especially formally, against the organization. With the advent and growth of labor unions, employees have gained tremendously in power, and the grievance procedure is a significant part of this power. A grievance is a formal dispute between management and an employee, or employees, over some condition of employment. The grievance procedure is a formal method for resolving grievances. Through the grievance procedure complaints are aired, ambiguities in the labor agreement are identified for settlement in future negotiations, and organizational policy is further defined. It should be realized that a nonunionized organization can have a grievance procedure. A grievance usually begins with an informal complaint by an employee. Often this complaint will be talked out between the employee and supervisor before it becomes a formal grievance. The supervisor should not be afraid of complaints. A reasonable number of complaints usually indicates a healthy atmosphere. Proper handling of complaints by the supervisor is extremely important. Once a complaint enters the formal grievance procedure, it will involve additional time, people, and costs to reach a decision.

The grievance procedure varies among organizations. Smaller organizations tend to have less formal procedures with fewer steps—usually one or two. Larger organizations have more formal procedures with more steps—typically three or four. The first step usually involves the complaining employee (called the grievant), the supervisor, and in the case of a union, the union steward. Subsequent steps involve higher levels of management and the union hierarchy. Arbitration is usually the final step in the process. Arbitration is a process by which both the union and management agree to abide by the decision of an outside party regarding the grievance. Figure 15–1 shows a typical grievance procedure involving a union.

Grievances arise for a wide variety of reasons. The most frequently encountered reasons involve disciplinary actions, promotions and layoffs, and distribution of work, including overtime. Some grievances are the result of a failure to abide by the union contract, law, or past practices of the organization. Other grievances result from a failure of the union contract to address the issue or the unclear nature of the contract and/or past practice concerning the issue. Regardless of the nature of the complaint, the grievance procedure provides a method for resolving the dispute.

FIGURE 15–1
Steps in a typical grievance procedure involving a labor union

1. The employee and union steward discuss the grievance with the supervisor.
2. Grievance is discussed by union grievance committee and supervisor's superior.
3. Grievance is considered by union grievance committee and manager of local organization and its industrial relations manager.
4. Grievance is discussed by national union representatives, union grievance committee, and organization's top general manager and industrial relations manager.
5. Grievance is discussed by national union representatives and top-management members.
6. Grievance is referred to mutually acceptable arbitrator for final decision.

There are many reasons for allowing the supervisor to settle the complaint before it enters the grievance procedure or at the lowest possible step of the grievance procedure. First, it saves time and money. Settling the grievance at the supervisory level saves the time of higher levels of management and the time of the union steward. Second, by achieving settlement prior to entering the formal grievance procedure, the employees' confidence in the supervisor's ability to make decisions and solve problems is enhanced. Many times an employee's attitude about the job and the organization is based on the relationship with the supervisor. Not only does early settlement develop the employee's confidence but it develops the confidence of higher levels of management in the supervisor's ability. Early settlement further develops confidence between management and the union in their ability to settle differences and avoid costly arbitration. Early settlement also prevents minor problems from becoming major disturbances that can upset morale and disrupt the entire organization.

Stressing pregrievance or early settlement of a complaint at the supervisory level does not suggest the supervisors should settle every complaint this way. Very unusual cases or decisions that could affect many employees should probably be referred to higher levels of management or the personnel department. An organization may be held accountable for its supervisors' decisions just as if the decision were made by the plant manager, the president, or the owner of the company. Grievances that result in the interpretation of broad general policies and union contract clauses should not generally be settled at the supervisory level.

Under no circumstances should the supervisor attempt to obstruct the grievance process. Many times the procedure acts as a safety valve, preventing more costly employee aggression.

HANDLING THE FIRST STEP OF
THE GRIEVANCE PROCESS

If the employee's complaint cannot be satisfied by an informal discussion with the supervisor, the complaint then becomes a formal grievance. In the first step of a formal grievance, the grievant and usually the union steward present the grievance to the supervisor. This grievance is usually described, in writing, on a grievance form. Written grievances not only establish a written record of the grievance, but they also tend to focus the discussion and investigation on the proper area. Another potential advantage of written grievances is that they may result in a grievance being dropped due to a lack of merit.

By the time the complaint has been formalized at the first step of the grievance procedure, the supervisor has usually had some discussion with the grievant. As in the pregrievance handling, the supervisor is advised to listen patiently and sympathetically to the grievant. If the supervisor does not have the time to listen to the grievance at the time it is first presented, a time should be scheduled as soon as possible to hear the grievant. The grievance should be treated seriously. The grievant should also be given the opportunity to state the problem without interruption other than occasional questions to help clarify the issue. Restating the complaint in summary and asking the grievant if the restatement represents a fair statement of the problem can be helpful in clarifying the issue. If necessary, the supervisor should ask the grievant and the steward for additional time to answer the grievance. However, every attempt should be made to abide by any time limits outlined in the union contract. The supervisor's objective should be to get all the facts. The more facts obtained, the more effective the supervisor's actions will be and the more receptive the grievant will be to the actions.

A supervisor must evaluate the facts objectively and attempt to determine the causes of the complaint. It is helpful to determine and evaluate alternative actions as to their cost and possible side effects. It is extremely important for the supervisor to maintain adequate records of all meetings with the grievant.

Once an evaluation has been made and the solution determined, the supervisor must plan the implementation of the solution. The grievant and the union steward should be informed of the solution and the reasons behind it before implementation begins. If the error was determined to be by management, the mistake should be admitted openly and a prompt settlement should be implemented. If the grievance is in management's favor, the supervisor should express confidence in the employee's willingness to abide by the decision.

Finally, the supervisor should follow up with frequent checks on the implementation of the solution. The supervisor must ensure that the adjustment was fair and did not create other problems.

The suggestions discussed in the preceding paragraphs should help the supervisor to minimize grievances and aid in settling them at the lowest possible level. The checklist provided in Figure 15–2 summarizes the steps that should be followed.

FIGURE 15–2
Checklist for minimizing grievances

1. Gain an understanding of the labor law, union contract, and past practice as it pertains to decisions made at the supervisory level.
2. Develop a cordial relationship with the union steward.
3. Provide a work environment that is as fair as possible.
4. Encourage openness.
5. Try to understand the opposing point of view.
6. Investigate the cause of the complaint.
7. Determine the issue.
8. Evaluate the facts objectively and determine the cause of the complaint.
9. Plan the implementation of the solution.
10. Advise operative and union personnel who will be affected by the solution before implementation.
11. Check frequently on the results and side effects of the solution.

Chapter 16

APPLYING DISCIPLINE

When a member of management wants to take an action against an operative employee for violating an organizational rule, the organization's disciplinary procedures are used. When an employee has a complaint against the organization or its management, the grievance procedure (which was discussed in the previous chapter) is normally used to solve the problem. Some organizations have a very formal discipline procedure; others are less formal; and some organizations have no formalized procedure at all. The purpose of this chapter is to outline typical disciplinary procedures and to suggest ways of positively using disciplinary actions.

A POSITIVE APPROACH TO DISCIPLINE

Discipline refers to the action imposed by an organization on its employees for failure to follow the rules, standards, or policies of the organization. Most organizations have some kind of disciplinary procedure, whether formal or informal, that carries successively stiffer penalties for repeated or more serious offenses. Figure 16–1 shows a suggested schedule of disciplinary steps that can be taken.

A formal discipline procedure usually begins with an oral warning that can progress througha written warning, suspension, and ultimately, discharge. Formal discipline procedures alsooutline the penalty for each successive offense and define time limits for maintaining records of

FIGURE 16–1
Suggested schedule of disciplinary steps

1. Oral warning that is not recorded in employee's personnel records.
2. Oral warning that is recorded in employee's personnel records.
3. Written reprimand.
4. Suspension.
5. Discharge.

each offense and penalty. For instance, tardiness records might be maintained for only a six-month time period. Tardiness prior to the six months preceding the offense would not be considered in the disciplinary action. Less formal agreements generally specify the reasons for disciplinary action as being for just cause, proper cause, or some other cause.

Preventing discipline from progressing beyond the warning step is obviously advantageous to both the employee and management. Discipline should be aimed at correction rather than at punishment. If the behavior can be corrected by a friendly talk between the supervisor and the employee, there is less chance of the situation becoming a source of bitterness. Similarly, formal oral or written warnings are less likely to cause animosity than a disciplinary suspension. It is obviously not in the supervisor's best interests to deprive employees of their income if the behavior can be corrected by an oral or written warning. A disciplinary suspension not only hurts the employee but also frequently deprives the supervisor and the organization of a needed employee. Of course, the most costly and least acceptable form of discipline is discharge. In most cases supervisors should make every effort to avoid discharging an employee. A supervisor should view discipline as a means of encouraging employees to willingly abide by the rules and standards of the organization.

HOW DOES A SUPERVISOR MAINTAIN GOOD DISCIPLINE?

One of the most important aspects of maintaining good discipline is communication. Employees cannot operate in an orderly and efficient manner unless they know the rules. The supervisor has the responsibility of informing employees of the rules, regulations, and standards of the organization. Informing employees of the rules is not always sufficient. The supervisor must also ensure that employees understand the purpose of the rules and regulations. It is also essential for employees to be reminded in a friendly manner when adherence to rules has become lax.

Counseling should, whenever possible, precede the use of disciplinary reprimands or stricter penalties. Through counseling the supervisor can uncover problems affecting human relations and productivity. Counseling further develops an environment of openness, understanding, and trust. This encourages employees to maintain self-discipline.

In order to maintain effective discipline, supervisors must always follow the rules that the employees are expected to follow. There is no justifiable reason for supervisors to bend the rules for themselves or for a favored employee. The employees must realize that the rules are for everyone. Supervisors should be fair toward all employees.

Although most employees follow the rules and regulations of the organization, there are times when a supervisor must use discipline. Figure 16–2 gives some frequent reasons for using discipline. A supervisor must not be afraid to use the disciplinary procedure when it becomes necessary. Failure to act may be interpreted by employees that the rule is not to be enforced. Supervisory decisions to discipline after a period of lax enforcement contribute to poor morale and reduced productivity. Failure to act can also frustrate the employees who are abiding by the rules. Properly applying discipline can also encourage borderline employees to improve their performance.

Before supervisors use the disciplinary procedure, they must be aware of how far they can go without involving higher levels of management. They must also determine how much union participation is required (if a union is present). If the employee who is to be disciplined is a member of a union, the contract may specify the penalty that must be used. Other requirements may also be specified by the contract, such as who must be present during a discipline meeting and the length of time a record of the discipline can be kept on the employee's record.

Because a supervisor's decision may be placed under critical review in the grievance process, a supervisor must be careful when applying discipline. Even if the supervisor is not functioning under a union agreement, most supervisors are subject to some review of their disciplinary actions. In order to avoid having a discipline decision rescinded at a higher level of management, it is important that the guidelines discussed below be followed.

PREDISCIPLINARY RECOMMENDATIONS

Every supervisor should attempt to become familiar with the law, union contract (if applicable), and past practices of the organization as they affect any disciplinary decisions. Supervisors should attempt

FIGURE 16–2
Reasons for disciplining employees

Absenteeism.
Tardiness.
Loafing.
Absence from work.
Leaving place of work (includes early quitting).
Sleeping on job.
Assault and fighting among employees.
Horseplay.
Insubordination.
Threat or assault of management representative.
Abusive language to supervisor.
Profane or abusive language (not toward supervisor).
Falsifying company records (including time records, production records).
Falsifying employment application.
Dishonesty.
Theft.
Disloyalty to government (security risk).
Disloyalty to employer (includes competing with employer, conflict of interest).
Moonlighting.
Negligence.
Damage to, or loss of, machinery or materials.
Incompetence (including low productivity).
Refusal to accept job assignment.
Refusal to work overtime.
Participation in prohibited strike.
Misconduct during strike.
Slowdown.
Union activities.
Possession or use of drugs.
Possession or use of intoxicants.
Obscene or immoral conduct.
Gambling.
Abusing customers.
Attachment or garnishment of wages.

Source: Adapted from Frank Elkouri and Edna Elkouri, *Arbitration Works,* 3d ed. (Washington, D.C.: Bureau of National Affairs, 1973), pp. 652–66.

to resolve any questions with higher management and the personnel department about their authority to discipline.

Maintaining adequate records cannot be overemphasized. Not only is it important to good supervision, but it can prevent a disciplinary decision from being rescinded. Written records often have a significant influence on decisions to overturn or uphold a disciplinary action. Past rule infractions and overall performance should also be recorded. A supervisor bears the burden of proof when a decision to discipline an employee is questioned. In cases where the charge is of a moral or criminal nature, the proof required is usually that which is required by a court of law (proof beyond a reasonable doubt). Adequate records by the supervisor and witnesses are of utmost importance in cases of this type. Noting good performance and improvement can also be helpful, especially in defending a charge of inconsistency by a disciplined employee.

Another key prediscipline responsibility is the investigation. That which appears obvious on the surface is sometimes completely discredited after investigation. Accusations against an employee must be supported by facts. Many decisions to discipline employees have been overturned due to an improper or less than thorough investigation. The supervisor must guard against undue haste in taking action when angry, or when there has not been a thorough investigation. Before disciplinary action is taken, the employee's motives and reasons for the rule infraction should be investigated and considered. The employee's work record should also be a prediscipline consideration. The investigation should take place prior to administering discipline. A supervisor should not discipline and then look for evidence to support the decision.

Furthermore, when the organization is unionized, the union should be kept informed on matters of discipline. Some organizations give unions advance notice of their intention to discipline an employee. Copies of warnings are sometimes also sent to the union.

ADMINISTERING FORMAL DISCIPLINE

A supervisor is expected to use progressive, corrective discipline. As has already been stated, it is to the supervisor's and organization's advantage to correct the employee's behavior with a minimum of discipline. Sometimes, however, counseling and friendly warnings are not sufficient and the employee must be formally reprimanded. A formal warning is not as likely to be reviewed by higher management and is less likely to produce resentment than a suspension or a discharge. There are still some key points that a supervisor should keep in mind when issuing a formal warning.

Applying discipline should be analogous to the burn received when touching a hot stove. Often referred to as the "hot stove rule," this approach emphasizes that discipline should be directed against the act rather than against the person. Other key points of the hot stove rule are immediacy, advance warning, consistency, and impersonality. Figure 16–3 illustrates the hot stove rule.

Immediacy refers to the length of time between the misconduct and the discipline. For discipline to be most effective, it must be taken as soon as possible but without making an emotional, irrational decision.

As has already been discussed, discipline should be preceded by advance warning. A supervisor cannot begin enforcing previously unenforced rules by disciplining an employee as an example. Notation of rules infractions in an employee's record is not sufficient to support disciplinary action. An employee must be advised of the infraction in order for it to be considered to be a warning. Noting that the employee was warned for the infraction and having the employee sign a discipline form are both good practices. Failure to warn an employee of the consequences of repeated violations of a rule is a reason often cited for overturning a disciplinary action.

A key element in discipline is consistency. Inconsistency lowers morale, diminishes respect for the supervisor, and leads to grievances. Striving for consistency does not mean that past infractions, length of service, work record, and other mitigating factors should not be

FIGURE 16–3
Hot stove rule for applying discipline

1. The hot stove burns immediately. Disciplinary policies should be administered quickly. There should be no question of cause and effect.
2. The hot stove gives a warning and so should discipline.
3. The hot stove consistently burns everyone that touches it. Discipline should be consistent.
4. The hot stove burns all in the same manner regardless of who they are. Discipline must be impartial. People are disciplined for what they have done and not because of who they are.

considered when applying discipline. However, an employee should feel that any other employee under essentially the same circumstances would have received the same penalty.

A supervisor should also take steps to ensure that personalities are not a factor when applying discipline. The employee should feel that the disciplinary action is a result of actions taken rather than personality factors or relationship to the supervisor. The supervisor should avoid arguing with the employee and should administer the discipline in a straightforward, calm manner. Administering discipline without anger or apology and resuming a pleasant relationship aids in reducing the negative personal effects of discipline.

The supervisor should also attempt to administer discipline in private. The only exception for public reprimand would be in the case of gross insubordination or flagrant and serious rule violations. In these situations a public reprimand might help the supervisor regain needed control. Even in these types of situations, the supervisor's objective should be to gain control and not to embarrass the employee.

Finally, the supervisor should warn the employee of the result of repeated violations. Sometimes suggestions to the employee on ways to correct behavior are beneficial.

SUSPENSIONS AND DISCHARGES

Supervisors should be very reluctant to impose disciplinary suspensions and discharges. Usually discipline of this degree is reserved for higher levels of management. Even if supervisors do not have the power to administer disciplinary suspensions or discharges, they often are the ones who make these recommendations to higher management. Since discipline of this nature is more likely to be reviewed, is more costly to the organization, and is more likely to be reflected in overall morale and productivity, it is very important for supervisors to know when this form of discipline should be recommended. Observing the hot stove rule is essential in administering suspensions and discharges.

A supervisor is expected to use corrective discipline whenever possible. There are, however, some offenses that may justify discharge. Some of these are stealing, striking a supervisor, and gross insubordination. The supervisor must be able to show, beyond a reasonable doubt, that the offense was committed. Attention to the points discussed in the prediscipline recommendations are especially important in supporting a decision to discharge an employee.

As in any lesser discipline, but even more essential in suspension and discharge, the employee has the right to a careful and impartial investigation. This involves allowing the employee to state his or her side of the case, to gather supporting evidence, and usually to question any accuser. In the case of very serious offenses, a supervisor may suspend the employee pending a full investigation. This may be necessary when an employee has been accused of a serious crime or something that could affect the safety of others.

The suggestions outlined in the preceding paragraphs should help the supervisor maintain discipline in a positive manner and with a minimum of application of the harsher forms of discipline. When the supervisor needs to apply the discipline procedure, observance of these suggestions should reduce the chance of a grievance, or if a grievance is filed, the chance of having the disciplinary action overruled. Figure 16–4 provides the supervisor with a checklist of rules that should be observed when applying discipline.

FIGURE 16–4
Supervisory checklist for applying discipline

1. Be familiar with the law, union contract (if applicable), and past practices of the organization as they affect the practice of discipline.
2. Maintain adequate records.
3. Investigate rule infractions and mitigating circumstances.
4. Keep union informed (if applicable).
5. Issue discipline as soon as possible.
6. Precede formal discipline with a warning.
7. Be consistent among employees.
8. Relate the penalty to the offense rather than to the person.
9. Administer discipline in private.
10. Warn of the results of a repeat violation.

Chapter 17

COST REDUCTION AND METHODS IMPROVEMENT

Reducing costs is a constant challenge to supervisors. Because many supervisory problems are directly related to cost, controlling costs helps to avoid other problems. Supervisors are in an ideal position to promote the objective of reducing operating costs because they have direct influence and control over many of them. The utilization of machines, the work methods to be followed, and the behavior of employees— all important considerations in the expenditures of any organization— are under the supervisor's direction. While staff specialists such as cost engineers and cost accountants may develop ways to measure and cut costs, it is usually the supervisor who actually engages directly in reducing the operating costs in a given department.

As is true with so many areas of supervision, the attitude of the supervisor toward costs sets the tone for the entire department. If the supervisor is cost conscious, it usually rubs off on the employees. The reverse of this is also true—if the supervisor has little concern for costs, the employees will seldom be concerned about costs. In addition to being cost conscious, the supervisor must be willing to listen to the cost-savings ideas of others.

FIGURING COSTS

Before supervisors can reduce costs they must know how to figure costs. Cost can be thought of as everything expended to provide the product or service. Generally these costs, as related to the supervisor, can be broken down into several categories.

1. Direct labor costs. These are expenditures for labor that are *directly* involved in the creation of the product or service. (The more product or service provided, the more direct labor that is used.) Examples include machine operators, claims processors, bank tellers, assembly-line workers, and salespeople.

2. Indirect labor costs. These are expenditures for labor that are not directly applied to the product or service. Examples include personnel specialists, quality control personnel, housekeeping personnel, and public relations specialists.

3. Operating supplies costs. These are expenditures for necessary items that do not become a part of the product or service (items in addition to the product/service raw materials). Examples include brochures explaining a service, cleaning compounds, safety clothing, and office supplies.

4. Maintenance costs. These include labor and material costs incurred to repair and maintain satisfactory performance of equipment and facilities. Examples include replacement parts, maintenance personnel, and repair bills.

5. Waste or scrap costs. These include products, parts or services that cannot be reworked or reused and that do not meet quality standards. Examples include items damaged during manufacture and unused services.

6. Energy costs. These include charges for electricity, gas, water, steam, and any other source of power.

7. Overhead costs. These include expenditures for physical space, staff services, research, advertising, and legal services. Generally, overhead costs are shared by several departments. Ordinarily an attempt is made to allocate these costs to each department on some equitable basis.

Depending on the degree of detail needed, each of the above major cost categories can be further broken down. For example, direct labor can be further categorized by shift or by section with the department. At the same time, however, this can be overdone. As a rule, cost information should be no more detailed than is necessary for making good decisions.

It is not unusual for supervisors to be provided with weekly or monthly cost reports for their departments based on the above cost categories. (See Figure 17–1 for an example.) These reports are usually prepared by the accounting department based on information provided by the supervisor. Naturally, these reports are no more accurate than the information provided by the supervisor. Therefore, supervisors should be sure that they understand what information is being sought.

Also, if supervisors do not understand any of the information on the report, they should seek clarification from the accounting department.

COST BUDGETS

A budget is a statement of expected results or requirements expressed in financial or numerical terms. Almost all supervisors must work with cost budgets. A supervisor's involvement with the cost-budgeting process can vary. In general, however, a supervisor should know how to develop a cost budget, how to operate within a budget, and how to use a budget for control. Even when a cost budget is dictated to a supervisor, it is helpful to understand the general process. The second column in Figure 17–1 represents the weekly budget for supervisor James Arnold.

Even when it is not required by upper management, it is wise for a supervisor to prepare cost budgets for each of the major cost categories (such as indirect labor, direct labor, operating supplies, etc.). Preparing a cost budget provides the supervisor with a goal to work toward. Referring again to Figure 17–1, supervisor James Arnold can readily identify those areas where he is experiencing cost problems (direct labor and supplies) and those areas that are in good shape (indirect labor, overtime, scrap, and utilities).

FIGURE 17–1
Sample cost report

Weekly cost report   Department No. 33
Week ending: March 10, 198*   Supervisor: James Arnold

Account	Budget	Actual	Over (For this week)	Under (For this week)	Over (Year to date)	Under (Year to date)	Comments
Direct labor	$2,900	$3,140	$240		$1,780		
Indirect labor	750	725		$ 25		$120	
Overtime	450	200		250		290	⎧ Made improve-
Scrap	400	390		10		70	⎪ ments this
Supplies	500	405		95	220		⎨ week but still
Utilities	125	137	12			15	⎪ over annual
Overhead	3,750	4,250	500		3,890		⎩ budget
Totals	$8,875	$9,247					

Typically, the supervisor plays a role in the organizational budgeting system. Budgeting systems normally start at the top levels of the organization and cascade down. Usually the supervisor participates in the preparation of the department's budget. The lower level budgets naturally must fit within the general constraints established from above. The common budget period is for one fiscal year, with breakdowns for quarterly and monthly periods. How often a budget is revised can vary depending on the system used. Under *periodic* budgeting, major revisions are made three times a year, in March, June, and September. The *progressive* approach calls for revisions every two months for the following six-month period. For example, at the end of February, revisions are made for the six-month period, March through August. A final method is the *moving* budget. Under a moving budget, revisions take place every month covering the next 12 months. In effect, one month is dropped and another is added in each revision.

The budgetary process should not be viewed as punitive, nor should it be used in a punitive manner. The purpose of a budget is not to punish or restrict a supervisor, but rather to aid. Properly used, a budget helps to accomplish realistic and specific goals within stated cost expenditures. Supervisors who master the budgeting process help themselves and their departments.

COST-REDUCTION GUIDELINES

Several guidelines should be followed when implementing a cost-reduction program. These are not presented as hard-and-fast rules, but rather as general guidelines to be followed.

1. Incentives should be offered as a reward for cost reduction. If employees believe that cost reduction is in their best interests, they are much more likely to actively participate. Some organizations allow employees to share in the cost savings realized; others give cash awards or time off to employees responsible for cost savings.

2. Cost reduction should be part of the normal routine. It should be regular and periodic and not a "once-a-year" effort. The goal is to develop a constant awareness of costs. All too often a brief intensive campaign is waged with some cost reduction achieved. However, shortly after the campaign has ended, costs once again begin to increase.

3. Cost reduction should be inclusive and cover all areas. It is not only ineffective, but also unfair, to permit costs to run wild in one area while being rigorously controlled in another area. One should remember that the *total* cost figure is the figure of most concern.

4. Individual responsibility for cost reduction should be made clear. One general problem with cost reduction is that when it's considered everybody's problem, it ends up being nobody's problem. Employees should be held responsible for costs under their control. At the same time, employees should be rewarded for controlling and reducing costs.

5. Make sure that the cost objectives are established. It is rather difficult to know what costs to work on controlling unless one knows what is and is not acceptable. It is also helpful to make sure that the responsible employees understand how these respective costs are calculated.

6. Be open to the use of a variety of techniques. Because different areas require different approaches, one technique does not work in all areas. A common problem occurs when a supervisor becomes attached to one particular technique and tries to apply it in all situations. The most successful approach is to match the technique or approach to the problem.

7. Supervisors should set the example. This was mentioned earlier, but it is important enough to repeat. The impression that supervisors give of their interest in cost reduction usually has a significant influence on the views of the employees. Supervisors should leave no doubt about their concern for cost reduction.

COST-REDUCTION STRATEGIES

Where should cost-reduction efforts be focused? Logically cost reduction should begin in those areas where the greatest savings can be realized. These areas are not always obvious. Locating them may require considerable effort, but such effort usually pays off. At the same time, small cost reductions are also important. This is especially true if the small reductions can be repeated frequently, thus adding up to a sizable reduction. With this in mind, several general strategies may be followed to cut costs. While all of the following strategies can be effective, the supervisor generally has more control over the first five than the last three.

1. Increase output. The idea here is to increase output utilizing the same or fewer resources. This reduces the cost per item of product or service. The supervisor should always try to operate at the level of output that results in the greatest efficiency. Unfortunately, supervisors are often drastically limited in this area in unionized situations.

2. Make better use of time. The focus here is on eliminating any unnecessary activities. This may involve the establishment of work standards and the improvement of work methods.

3. Regulate or level the work flow. A regular, steady flow with no bottlenecks and no equipment breakdowns is desirable. Irregular flows with many peaks and valleys are usually inefficient and often require the use of costly overtime.

4. Minimize waste. The creation of unnecessary services and the scrapping of partially processed or unused materials can be very expensive. Any effort to reduce these wastes can pay big dividends. Other types of waste include idle personnel, work expended on projects of little value, and equipment not being used at full capacity. For example, the supervisor of a cafeteria should carefully plan the quantities of the different foods to prepare so as to minimize the amount of leftovers.

5. Analyze all control points. Adequate control is not only desirable but necessary. However, excessive control can interfere with the work and run up costs. For instance, quality checks should be properly spaced to ensure the desired quality but should not be overdone to the point of interfering with the accomplishment of the work.

6. Ensure adequate storage space is available. Inadequate storage can be quite costly. This situation can cause unnecessary materials handling and production delays. In a service-oriented organization, storage space would include such things as adequate waiting rooms and adequate space for storing supplies.

7. Install modern equipment. Obsolete and worn-out equipment should be replaced. This not only increases the machine efficiency, but it usually has a positive effect on the operator. For example one has only to look at the improvements that have been made in the typewriter field (a manual typewriter versus a modern word processor).

8. Invest in employee training. Employees who properly understand their jobs are more efficient than those who don't. Usually any front-end investments in training are made up through increased job efficiency.

Supervisors seeking to cut costs will invariably spot some possibilities. The key is to look for them. At the same time, however, supervisors should not fail to use all available resources. Staff specialists can be very helpful. Cost analysts, industrial engineers, and others on the staff can offer expertise in certain areas. Also, the ideas of the employees should not be overlooked. The person who does the job every day generally has some good ideas about how it can be improved. The key is to listen and evaluate all suggestions. It is also important to implement worthwhile suggestions and to give recognition to the employees who make them. A final resource is a cost-reduction committee. A cost-reduction committee offers the benefits of group thinking. It also helps to raise the consciousness of the committee members to the idea of cost reduction.

WHY DO EMPLOYEES FEAR COST REDUCTION?

It is only natural for employees to feel threatened by cost reduction. Loss of overtime, reduction of regular working hours, job loss, and fear of being "slave driven" are some of the more obvious fears. One way to help eliminate these fears is to encourage employee participation in reducing costs. The first step is to present the facts in an understandable manner to the employees. Once this has been accomplished, the employees should be given an opportunity to ask questions and receive feedback. After a decision has been made, the reasons for the decision and the methods to be used should be communicated to the employees. It is important that this information be communicated as soon as possible to head off any potential rumors.

Another important thing is to make sure that some type of payoff is available to the employees who participate in reducing costs. As mentioned earlier, employees who believe that they will benefit by reducing costs are naturally going to be more concerned about costs than those who don't.

Unfortunately, cost reduction has gotten a bad name in many instances because a supervisor has mismanaged a cost-reduction program. The result is often to turn off employees to the whole idea of cost control. More often than not, this mismanagement has occurred out of neglect more than anything else. Successful cost reduction and control require a conscientious effort on the part of the supervisor.

IMPROVING WORK METHODS

One of the most effective ways of reducing costs is by improving work methods. The overriding objective when improving work methods is to find the "one best way" of performing a particular job. Work-methods improvement has been called the organized application of common sense to find easier and better ways of doing work by the elimination of waste of any kind including energy, time, space, material, and equipment. *Methods engineering* and *work simplification* are other terms that refer to the same process as work-methods improvement. Work-methods improvement is used to find the most efficient way to achieve a given task. The old saying, "Work smarter, not harder" sums up the objective of work-methods improvement.

METHODS IMPROVEMENT AND THE SUPERVISOR

Most supervisors want to get more and better output at lower cost in shorter time. Methods improvement is used to help achieve this objective. The supervisor's vantage point allows the areas that need methods improvements to be spotted. Not only do most supervisors have an overall view of what is going on, they also have close contact with the work.

The supervisor can create an environment that encourages methods improvements on the part of the employees. First and foremost, the employees must be given the tools and know-how for simplifying work. While many methods improvements are based on common sense, certain tools are available that can greatly aid in the process. Second, the employees must be motivated to make methods improvements. The supervisor can create an improvement-oriented atmosphere by actively listening and following up on employee suggestions and by rewarding employees for methods improvements. Employees quickly detect a supervisor who is reluctant to listen and try suggested ideas.

Of course, none of the above will work unless the supervisor is a true believer in methods improvement. The supervisor should set the example. A supervisor should never lose sight of the fact that *all work can be improved.* The key is to concentrate on those areas which have the greatest potential for payoff. Aside from actively participating in methods improvements, the supervisor should periodically talk up the subject with employees and encourage them to attend available methods-improvement training programs. In the final analysis, employees will react to their perceptions of the supervisor. If they believe that methods improvement is important to the supervisor, it will be important to them. If they believe that methods improvement is not important to the supervisor, then it will not be important to them.

SYSTEMATIC METHODS IMPROVEMENT

Regrettably, many supervisors look on methods improvement as something that occurs naturally. These beliefs are based on the assumption that any tasks or jobs warranting methods improvement are generally obvious. This is often not the case. As with most any endeavor, a conscious and organized approach to methods improvement produces the best results. A systematic approach to methods improvement consists of the following six steps.

Step 1: Select the task or job to be improved. As we discussed previously, all work can be improved. At the same time, it only makes good sense to direct improvements to areas that will probably produce the greatest results. Determining the areas most likely to produce the greatest results is not always easy. There are certain indicators, however, that supervisors should learn to look for and recognize. The key is to consciously look for these indicators. Jobs involving a lot of people, where waste or scrap is high, where materials are expensive, and where labor costs are highest, are usually fruitful areas for methods improvement. Other indicators to look for include production or customer bottlenecks, extensive overtime, excessive delays, and employee boredom. Also, jobs having repetitive operations usually have potential for substantial savings.

Step 2: Gather data on the selected jobs. After a job has been selected for improvement, the next step is to gather data about the job. This involves a careful analysis of the job. Performance can be observed critically and pertinent questions asked, and notes can be carefully kept. To help get all the facts and to aid in subsequent analysis, a flow process chart is commonly used.

A flow process chart shows, from top to bottom, the successive detailed steps in work performance. Each step is noted on a separate line, with a brief statement about it and its identifying symbol. The chart can be drawn for either the operator or the material as the reference subject, but the same subject must be used throughout.

Figure 17–2 shows a portion of a flow process chart in which the work deals with the assembly of a component. The first step is to pick up a plate with the left hand. This is known as an "operation" and is identified by the symbol of a large circle that is filled in solid on the chart. In addition to the circle, there are the following symbols: (1) an arrow for transportation or movement from one location to

FIGURE 17-2
Flow process chart

		No. 67 B	Page No. 1	Number of Pages 1 of 1

Process Part Z 942 C-1 Assembly		Actions	Summary					
			Present		Proposed		Difference	
☑ Man or ☐ Material			No.	Time	No.	Time	No.	Time
		○ Operations	5	.47				
Chart Begins Employee at Workbench	Chart Ends Employee at Workbench	⇨ Transportations	1	.20				
		☐ Inspections	1	.10				
Charted by C.M. Sullivan	Date May 4, 197—	D Delays	3	.15				
		▽ Storages						
Organization Parts 21		Distance Traveled (feet)		25				

Step No.	Details of Method ☑ Present ☐ Proposed	Operation	Transportation	Inspection	Delay	Storage	Distance (in feet)	Quantity	Time	Analysis (why?) What? Where? When? Who? How?	Notes	Analysis Change Eliminate Combine Sequence Place Person Improve
1	Pick up plate with L/hand	●	⇨	☐	D	▽	1	1	.08	✓ ✓		
2	Pick up washer with R/hand and center over hole in plate	●	⇨	☐	D	▽	1	1	.08	✓ ✓		
3	Hold partial assembly in L/hand	○	⇨	☐	D	▽	-	-	.05	✓✓ ✓		
4	Pick up bolt with R/hand and slide in hole in plate	●	⇨	☐	D	▽	1	1	.08	✓ ✓		
5	Hold partial assembly in L/hand	○	⇨	☐	D	▽	-	-	.05	✓✓ ✓		
6	Pick up lock washer with R/hand and slip over end of bolt	●	⇨	☐	D	▽	1	1	.08	✓ ✓		
7	Hold partial assembly in L/hand	○	⇨	☐	D	▽	-	-	.05	✓✓ ✓		
8	Pick up nut with R/hand and twist on end of bolt	●	⇨	☐	D	▽	1	1	.15	✓ ✓		
9	Look over assembly to see if it is O.k.	○	⇨	☐	D	▽	-	-	.10	✓✓	Is this necessary?	
10	Place assembly in box 10 ft. to operator's left	○	⇨	☐	D	▽	20	1	.20	✓ ✓		
		○	⇨	☐	D	▽						
		○	⇨	☐	D	▽						
		○	⇨	☐	D	▽						
		○	⇨	☐	D	▽						
		○	⇨	☐	D	▽						
		○	⇨	☐	D	▽						
		○	⇨	☐	D	▽						
		○	⇨	☐	D	▽						
		○	⇨	☐	D	▽						
		○	⇨	☐	D	▽						
		○	⇨	☐	D	▽						

another, (2) a square for inspection, (3) a D for delay or temporary stoppage, and (4) a triangle with the point down for storage.

Step 3: Analyze and question each step of the job. Having collected data concerning the way the job is currently being done, the steps then need to be analyzed and evaluated. The necessity of *each* step should be questioned. Why is this step necessary? What would be the cost of eliminating this step? The flow process chart developed in Step 2 can be used to help spot inefficiencies and eliminate unnecessary steps. Remember, the overriding purpose of this step is to identify inefficient work and wasted motions.

Step 4: Develop improved method or methods. As a result of the questioning in Step 3, many possibilities for improving the work methods may have surfaced. The purpose of Step 4 is to examine these possibilities, to develop others, and then to determine which possibilities are the best.

The best method for performing a job is a function of (1) how the human body is used, (2) the arrangement of the work place, and (3) the design of the equipment used. It is often possible to make improvements in one or more of these components and in the manner in which they are put together. Improvements can usually be made by eliminating, combining, rearranging, and simplifying the steps of the job. Logically, only some of the improvements that emerge can be used. The objective is to determine which of the improvements are the best.

Step 5: Obtain approval for improvement. Developing an improvement is frequently not sufficient. Many times others in the organization must be convinced that the improvement is sound. Approval is often necessary if a change in policy or product design is involved. It is similarly often wise to keep the boss informed as a new method or procedure is being developed. Care must be taken in presenting and justifying a proposal. An acceptable proposal includes a brief description, what it will accomplish, how it will work, how much it will save, what it will cost, and what effect it will have on the employees. It is usually desirable to put the proposal in writing. This gives the boss the pertinent data needed to make a final decision. It also shows that the improvement has been thoroughly studied.

Step 6: Install improvement and follow-up. Approval of the improvement does not end the process. The improvement must be put into operation. Acceptance of the improvement and cooperation of the affected employees are mandatory. Employees naturally resist change if they have not been involved in the process. Therefore, employees should be involved as much as possible in any methods-improvement program. Any changes should be carefully explained along with the reasons for the changes. Ideas for implementing a change should be actively solicited from the employees. The affected employees must receive thorough training in the improved method and on any new equipment.

After the improvement has been introduced, it is wise to periodically follow up and make sure that no difficulties developed. Minor adjustments may be required to make things run smoothly. Checks should be made to see that the new method is producing the expected results.

A NOTE OF CAUTION

When undertaking any type of methods-improvement program, a supervisor should always give proper attention to the affected employees. As discussed in the previous section, employees naturally resist change if they are not involved in the change. Also, the content of the job must always be considered. A job can be oversimplified to the point of being boring. Such a situation can adversely affect employee motivation and employee productivity. A successful methods-improvement program should be concerned with finding the best method for performing a task or group of tasks. This involves eliminating *unnecessary* work. However, it does not necessarily mean that the task or job should be restructured in scope as much as possible. Similarly, it is *not* the objective of methods improvement to make the task or job as simple as possible. The objective is to increase efficiency through the elimination of unnecessary work and through the optimal structuring of necessary work.

Chapter 18

SAFETY AND THE SUPERVISOR

Safety is an important problem for today's organizations. During 1978 approximately 1 out of every 11 American workers in the private sector suffered an injury or illness caused by exposure to hazards in the work environment. This resulted in approximately 2.25 million lost workdays for employers with 11 or more employees. In this same year approximately 5,000 work-related deaths occurred for employers with 11 or more employees. The costs of work-related accidents to American industry are known to be in the billions of dollars annually.

The supervisor is the key person in any safety program. The degree to which the supervisor promotes safe practices determines the effectiveness of the department's safety programs. Thus, supervision and safety go hand in hand. A part of every supervisor's responsibility is to implement the company's safety program, making certain that the department's work area is safe and that the employees are working safely.

THE CAUSES OF ACCIDENTS

Accidents do happen; no one is automatically exempt from them. Cuts, burns, scalds, smashed fingers, broken ribs, bruised legs, electric shock—all can afflict employees. Some accidents leave permanent scars or handicaps; others even prove fatal.

There is a cause for every accident, and some lack or failure must be corrected to prevent a recurrence. Tripping and falling on the hall floor is not a cause, it is a result—an accident. The cause may have been inadequate lighting, an obstacle erroneously left on the floor, or the injured person's failure to watch where he or she was walking.

Accidents generally are the result of a combination of circumstances and events. The circumstances and events causing accidents usually result from either unsafe personal acts or an unsafe physical environment or both.

PERSONAL ACTS

Most experts believe that unsafe personal acts cause the bulk of organizational accidents. In fact, unsafe personal acts have been estimated by some to cause 80 percent of all organizational accidents. Unsafe personal acts include such things as taking unnecessary chances, horseplay, failing to wear protective equipment, using improper tools and equipment, and taking unsafe shortcuts.

It is difficult to determine why employees commit unsafe personal acts. There probably is no precise reason. Fatigue, haste, boredom, stress, poor eyesight, daydreaming, and physical inabilities are all potential reasons. However, these reasons do not explain why employees intentionally neglect to wear prescribed equipment or don't follow proper procedures. Most employees think of accidents as always happening to someone else. Such an attitude can easily lead to carelessness or a lack of respect for what can happen. It is also true that some people get a kick out of taking chances and showing off to others.

A poor safety record can adversely affect employee morale. The reverse of this is also true. Low employee morale can adversely affect the safety record. Research studies have shown that employees with low morale tend to have more accidents than employees with high morale. This is not surprising when one considers that low morale is likely to be related to employee carelessness.

THE PHYSICAL ENVIRONMENT

Accidents can and do happen in all types of environments. Accidents can happen in offices and retail stores just as they can in factories and lumber yards. There are, however, certain places where accidents occur most frequently. These are listed in order of decreasing frequency:

1. Wherever heavy, awkward material is handled, using hand trucks, forklift trucks, cranes, and hoists. About one third of organizational accidents are caused by handling and lifting material. Improper lifting by humans is also a frequent cause of accidents.

2. Around any type of machinery that is used to produce something else. Among the more hazardous are metal and woodworking machines, power saws, and machines with exposed gears, belts, chains, and the like. Even a paper cutter or an electric pencil sharpener has a high-accident potential.

3. Wherever human beings walk or climb, including ladders, scaffolds, and narrow walkways. Falls are a major source of organizational accidents.

4. Wherever people use hand tools, including chisels, screwdrivers, pliers, hammers, and axes. Hand tools also account for a good many household accidents.

5. Wherever electricity is used in addition to usual lighting sources. Among the places where electrical accidents occur are near extension cords, loose wiring, and portable hand tools. Outdoor power lines have a high-accident potential.[1]

Just as there are certain places where accidents occur more frequently, there are also certain physical conditions that seem to result in more accidents. Some of these unsafe physical conditions are:

1. Unguarded or improperly guarded machines (such as an unguarded belt).
2. Poor housekeeping (such as congested aisles, dirty or wet floors, and improper stacking of materials).
3. Defective equipment and tools.
4. Poor lighting.
5. Poor or improper ventilation.
6. Improper dress (such as wearing clothes with loose and floppy sleeves when working near a rotating machine).

Figure 18–1 summarizes some specific safety hazards that frequently result in accidents.

FIGURE 18–1
Some specific safety hazards

1. Slippery floors.
2. Loose tile, linoleum, or carpeting.
3. Small loose objects left lying on the floor.
4. Bottles, cans, and books on the floor or stacked on top of filing cabinets or windowsills.
5. Sharp burrs on edges of material.
6. Reading while walking.
7. Cluttered aisles and stairs.

---

[1] Gary Dessler, *Personal Management: Modern Concepts and Techniques* (Reston, Va.: Reston, 1978), p. 426.

ACCIDENT PRONENESS

A third reason often given for accidents is "that certain people are accident prone." There is little doubt that some employees, due to their physical and mental makeup, are more susceptible to accidents. This condition may result from inborn traits, but often it develops as a result of the individual's environment. However, accident proneness should not be used to justify an accident. Employees who appear to be accident prone should be identified and receive special attention. Given the right set of circumstances, anyone can be accident prone. For example, a very "normal" employee who was up all night with a sick child might very well be "accident prone" the next day. Thus, those employees who have temporary accident proneness should also receive attention.

HOW TO MEASURE SAFETY

Accident frequency and accident severity are the two most widely accepted methods for measuring an organization's safety record. *A frequency rate indicates the frequency with which disabling injuries occur. A severity rate indicates how severe the accidents were.* A severity rate shows the length of time the injured parties were out of work. Only disabling injuries are used in determining frequency and severity rates. Disabling injuries are injuries that cause the employee to miss one or more days of work following the accident. Disabling injuries are also known as "lost-time injuries." Figure 18–2 gives the formulas for calculating the frequency rate and severity rate.

Neither the frequency rate or the severity rate mean much until

FIGURE 18–2
Formulas for computing accident frequency rate and severity rate

$$\text{Frequency rate} = \frac{\text{Number of disabling injuries} \times 1,000,000}{\text{Total number of labor-hours worked each year}}$$

$$\text{Severity rate} = \frac{\text{Days lost* due to injury} \times 1,000,000}{\text{Total number of labor-hours worked each year}}$$

* The American National Standards Institute has developed tables for determining the number of lost days for different types of accidents. To illustrate, an accident resulting in death or permanent total disability is charged with 6,000 days (approximately 25 working years).

they are compared with similar figures. Useful comparisons can be made with other departments or divisions within the organization, with previous years' figures, or with comparative figures of other organizations. It is through these comparisons that an organization's safety record can be objectively evaluated.

THE SAFETY PROGRAM

The heart of any organizational safety program is accident prevention. It is obviously much better to prevent accidents than to react to them. A major objective of any safety program is to get the employees to "think safety." Therefore, most safety programs are designed to keep safety and accident prevention on the employee's mind. There are many different and varied approaches used to make employees more aware of safety. However, four basic elements are present in most successful safety programs. First, the safety program must have the support of top and middle management. This support must be genuine and not casual. If upper management takes an unenthusiastic approach to safety, the employees will be quick to pick up on this. Second, it must be clearly established that safety is a line organization responsibility. All line managers should consider safety an integral part of their jobs. Furthermore, the operative employee also has a responsibility for working safely. Third, a positive attitude toward safety must exist and be maintained. The employees must believe that the safety program is worthwhile and that it produces results. Finally, there should be a person in charge of the safety program and responsible for its operation. Typically, this is the safety engineer or the safety director but it might also be a high-level line manager or the personnel manager.

THE SUPERVISOR'S RESPONSIBILITY FOR SAFETY

A successful safety program starts at the very top of the organization. The owners, top executives, and middle managers must all be committed to safety. However, because supervisors are the representatives of management who have daily contact with the employees, they are the key people in the program. Although supervisors often do not develop the safety procedures and rules, they are the ones who must see that they are followed. Even in organizations that have a safety engineer or a safety director, supervisors have responsibility for seeing that the safety directives are carried out. It is from supervisors that the employees take their cue as to what is and what is not important. It is the supervisors who shape the employees' attitude toward safety. Because supervisors are responsible for the safety of their employees, they should listen attentively to employee complaints relating to safety. These complaints should always be checked out and corrective action taken when necessary. Supervisors also should strive to develop good working relationships with the safety engineer or safety director (if one exists). The safety engineer or safety director should be consulted on any safety-related problems that come up. These actions can help to head off many accidents before they occur.

Supervisors should work to develop good relations with the safety committee (if one exists). Most safety committees are composed of operative employees and representatives of management. The committee's normal duties include inspecting and observing work practices, investigating, and making safety recommendations. Supervisors who don't utilize their safety committees are wasting a good resource. The safety committee can provide help in achieving safety goals. Also, safety committees usually only act in an advisory capacity. Supervisors are responsible for carrying out the committee's recommendations. Thus, supervisors and safety committees are really dependent on each other.

Safety instruction should be an integral part of orienting and training employees. Most supervisors have an active role in this process. Employees cannot be expected to use safe methods if they don't know what they are. Clear instructions regarding safety methods and procedures should be a part of every orientation program.

In addition to the general responsibilities described above, supervisors may also be responsible for such things as accident investigation, first aid, maintenance of proper safety records, and the dissemination of any changes in safety regulations and methods.

HOW THE SUPERVISOR CAN PREVENT ACCIDENTS

Because supervisors are the link between management and the operative employees, they are in the best position to effect safety. As previously discussed, the attitude presented by supervisors toward safety often sets the tone for how the employees view safety. In addition to fostering a healthy attitude toward safety, there are several specific things that supervisors can do to prevent accidents:

1. Make the work interesting. Making the work interesting is an effective way of preventing accidents. Uninteresting work can lead to boredom, fatigue, and stress, all of which can cause accidents.

2. Be familiar with organizational policies that relate to safety. Make sure the appropriate policies are conveyed to the employees.

3. Be familiar with the proper procedures for safely accomplishing the work. See that all employees know the proper method for doing their jobs. (This is equally applicable to both old and new employees.)

4. Know what safety devices and personal protective equipment should be used on each job. Insure that the respective jobholders use the proper safety devices and wear the proper protective equipment.

5. Know what safety-related reports and records are required (such as accident reports, investigation reports, etc.). Be sure that these reports are completed and processed on a timely basis.

6. Get to know the employees. Learn to identify both permanent and temporary accident prone employees. Once these employees have been identified, be sure that they receive proper attention.

7. Know when and where to make safety inspections. It is generally wise to develop a schedule for making safety inspections. This ensures that they won't be neglected.

8. Learn to take the advice of the safety director and the safety committee. Look on both of these groups as resources. Learn to work closely with these resources.

9. Know what to do in the case of an accident. Be familiar with basic first aid, know how to contact the doctor, ambulance, and hospital.

10. Know the proper procedures for investigating an accident and determining how it could have been prevented. Know the proper procedures to follow during an investigation.

11. Always set a good example with regard to safety. Remember the employees are always watching the supervisor.

THE OCCUPATIONAL SAFETY AND HEALTH ACT (OSHA)

In 1970 Congress passed the Occupational Safety and Health Act (OSHA), which became effective on April 28, 1971. Its stated purpose is to assure safe and healthy working conditions for every employee. The Occupational Safety and Health Administration of the U.S. Department of Labor enforces this act which covers all businesses in commerce with one or more employees. (There are certain exceptions such as businesses employing only family.) Under the act, the Occupational Safety and Health Administration is authorized to do the following:

> Encourage employers and employees to reduce work place hazards and to implement new or improved existing safety and health programs.
>
> Establish "separate but dependent responsibilities and rights" for employers and employees for the achievement of better safety and health conditions.
>
> Maintain a reporting and record-keeping system to monitor job-related injuries and illnesses.
>
> Develop mandatory job safety and health standards and enforce them effectively.
>
> Provide for the development, analysis, evaluation, and approval of state occupational safety and health programs.

Few laws have evoked as much reaction as OSHA. While few people would question the intent of OSHA, many have criticized the manner in which the act has been implemented. The sheer volume of regulations is staggering. Another frequent criticism is the vague wording of many OSHA regulations. As an example, the Occupational Safety and Health Administration developed the following 39-word, single-sentence definition of the word *exit:*

> That portion of a means of egress which is separated from all other spaces of the building or structure by construction or equipment as required in this subject to provide a protected way of travel to the exit discharge.[2]

OSHA has similarly been criticized as being overly petty with regard to many of its regulations. For example, one regulation states, "Where working clothes are provided by the employer and become wet or are washed between shifts, provision shall be made to insure that such clothing is dry before reuse."

Because of definitions and regulations similar to the above examples, many organizations have developed a negative attitude toward OSHA.

---

[2] Hugh Sidney, "Trying to Regulate the Regulations," *Time,* Dec. 5, 1977, p. 33.

As a result of this, recent legislation has been proposed to soften some of the OSHA requirements. Also, many of the original OSHA standards have been revoked by the Occupational and Health Administration itself.

THE SUPERVISOR AND OSHA

While impacting on the entire organizations, OSHA also places certain responsibilities on the supervisor. OSHA requires that the supervisor keep very specific records. These include (1) OSHA Form 200 (Log and Summary of Occupational Injuries and Illnesses). Each recordable occupational injury and illness must be recorded on this form within six working days from the time the employer learns of the accident or illness. (2) OSHA Form 101 (Supplementary Record of Occupational Injuries and Illness). This form contains much more detail about each injury or illness that has occurred. It must also be completed within six working days from the time the employer learns of the accident or illness. Only those injuries and illnesses resulting in deaths, lost workdays, loss of consciousness, restriction of work or motion, transfer to another job, or medical treatment (other than first aid) must be reported. Injuries requiring temporary first aid do not have to be recorded. Substitute forms are allowed for both Form 200 and Form 101 under certain conditions.

Supervisors are frequently asked to accompany OSHA officials while they inspect an organization's physical facilities. Because many organizations and supervisors feel threatened by an OSHA inspection, it is natural to want to be antagonistic. However, it is in the best interests of the supervisor and the host organization for the supervisor to be cooperative with the OSHA officials. An uncooperative supervisor could cause OSHA officials to be more hard-nosed than usual. The end result could be stiffer penalties imposed by OSHA.

Supervisors should be familiar with the OSHA regulations affecting their departments. They should constantly be on the lookout for safety violations. As previously discussed, it is the supervisor's responsibility to see that all safety rules are followed by the employees. This would naturally include all OSHA rules and regulations.

Chapter 19

ETHICS AND ORGANIZATIONAL POLITICS

Ethics are standards or principles of conduct used to govern the behavior of an individual or group of individuals. Ethics are generally concerned with questions relating to what is right or wrong or with moral duties. The behavior of supervisors, what goals they seek, and what actions they take are all affected by ethics. In any given situation what is perceived as "right" naturally affects the supervisor's actions and the actions of employees.

Moral standards are the result of social forces and human experiences over hundreds of years. For example, society condemns cheating, lying, and stealing. However, the application of ethics is an individual consideration. Do you or do you not follow moral standards when dealing with others? Are you aware of the moral code and if so, how do you interpret it?

Differences in awareness and interpretation of ethical standards create many problems. To illustrate, when does an action leave honorable self-interest and become legal dishonesty? Does the fact that a person was not disciplined for a certain action make it acceptable?

All too often actions are justified based on the means used or on the ends accomplished. That is, was the act morally right based on the means used, or should it be viewed as right based on the end result? On might reason, for example, that the act of lying was right because it achieved positive results. Conversely one might consider any action that involves ethical means to be perfectly justifiable regardless of the outcome. The problem is that this type of logic can be used to justify almost any action.

Because of the problems outlined above, fixed moral standards are called for in organizations. Supervisors should have fixed moral standards and abide by them.

SETTING THE TONE

Supervisors must set the example. Subscribing to the theory of "Do what I say, not what I do" doesn't work. Employees are much more impressed by what supervisors do than by what they say.

The supervisor sets the ethical tone of the work setting. The employees take their cue as to what is acceptable and not acceptable from the supervisor's actions. If the supervisor is perceived as being slightly unethical or dishonest, then employees are likely to feel that similar behavior on their part is acceptable. For example, if the employees have reason to believe that the supervisor is "borrowing" things from the storeroom, they may not see anything wrong with doing the same thing. On the other hand, some might still feel that it is wrong and lose respect for the supervisor.

In addition, a supervisor's general attitude toward ethics can also greatly affect employee ethics. Failure to take corrective action in certain situations also affects the ethical tone. Failure to act on the part of a supervisor is often interpreted by the employees as condonement.

AREAS REQUIRING ETHICAL CONDUCT BY SUPERVISORS

Many areas of supervision require ethical conduct. While some areas are more obvious than others, most can be grouped into three general categories: (1) loyalty, (2) human relations, and (3) covert personal action.

Loyalty. The category of loyalty has to do with where supervisors loyalties lie. Do the supervisors place their own interests ahead of everything else, or are they dedicated to the goals and needs of the employees, the organization, their families, or others? Regardless of the leadership displayed, the communication skills used, or the general knowledge present, supervisors will not have effective influence unless their own objectives are viewed positively by the employees. Supervisors who are perceived as being only interested in themselves and their future have difficulty in getting the full cooperation of the employees.

Human relations. This category centers around supervisors' concepts of fairness. It is concerned with how supervisors treat other people, especially subordinates. Ethics play a major role in determining how supervisors treat their subordinates. Are all of the supervisors' interper-

FIGURE 19–1
Examples of ethical conduct required of supervisors

Loyalty	Human relations	Covert personal actions
Has concern for employee welfare.	Deals honestly with employees.	Doesn't cut corners to save time.
Has concern for company welfare.	Shows empathy when called for.	Concerned with employee safety.
Has concern for family.	Objectively evaluates employees.	Never tries to cheat the company out of something.
Takes credit only when deserved.	Fairly disciplines employees.	Is well thought of in the community.

sonal dealings honest or do supervisors have a tendency to talk behind people's backs? Do supervisors treat their employees fairly or do they play favorites? Do supervisors deceive their peers in order to make them look bad?

Covert personal actions. The category of covert personal actions includes all other actions taken by supervisors that might reflect their ethics. These actions may be both internal or external to the organization. Internal actions would include such things as not circumventing organizational policy. External actions would include such things as how supervisors behave in the community. Figure 19–1 gives several specific examples of the different areas of ethical conduct required by supervisors.

ORGANIZATIONAL POLITICS

Organizational politics refers to the practice of using means other than merit or good performance for bettering your position or gaining favor in the organization. Organizational politics includes such things as trying to influence the boss, trying to gain power, and trying to gain a competitive edge over your peers. Self-interest is usually the motivating force behind organizational politics. Depending on the method used, organizational politics can involve unethical behavior. This occurs when individuals pursue their own self-interest to the point of harming others or the organization. Almost any approach to organiza-

FIGURE 19–2
**How to improve your political position within
the organization**

1. Know your boss.
2. Know how to keep your boss happy.
3. Be loyal.
4. Show respect for your boss.
5. Seize opportunities to make your boss look good.
6. Avoid antagonizing other departments.
7. Insist on feedback from your boss.
8. Help take the load off the boss.
9. Build a power base with your subordinates.
10. Seek responsibility and authority.
11. Gain the respect of subordinates.
12. Get people obligated to you.

tional politics can be ethical or unethical depending on how it is used by the individual. Figure 19–2 lists several things that supervisors can do to improve their political position within the organization.

DEALING WITH DISHONEST SUBORDINATES AND PEERS

How does a supervisor deal with dishonest subordinates and peers? This is really two questions, since peers must be handled somewhat differently from subordinates. With regard to subordinates, the supervisor must first build a case. The supervisor must gather proof of the subordinate's dishonesty. This does not mean taking the word of others. It means carefully documenting the available evidence. For example, if an employee is suspected of stealing from the supply cabinet, care should be taken to document what was missing and when it was missed. The employee's whereabouts during these times should also be documented. Once the supervisor is confident of having the facts, the employee should be confronted concerning the problem. The organization's disciplinary system should then be followed. The keys here are (1) get the facts and document the case, (2) confront the employee, and (3) follow the established disciplinary system.

The approach to dealing with peers is somewhat different from that of dealing with subordinates. The relationships involved are significantly different. Also, you may not be in a position to deal directly with the problem. For example, as a supervisor you may suspect that another supervisor is dishonest. However, because you and the suspected supervisor work in different areas, you may never be in a position to prove or disprove your suspicions. In this case, you should not jump to conclusions but rather simply deal cautiously with this person. If you do work in the same area as the suspected peer, you should carefully gather the facts and document your case. When you are confident that you have adequate facts to support your position, you should present them to your boss.

DEALING WITH AN "IMPOSSIBLE" BOSS

Unfortunately there are bosses in this world who shouldn't be managing others. Impossible bosses fall into several categories: (1) incompetent but nice persons, (2) mean for the sake of being mean, (3) lazy, and (4) laissez-faire, or just don't care. Because each of these impossible bosses must be dealt with differently, the first step is to identify the type of boss in question. But regardless of the category, of "impossible boss," it is not wise to go around talking about him or her. Such activities always seem to get back to the boss.

Incompetent but nice bosses. Those bosses who are nice but incompetent are often simply in over their heads. These persons usually are the victims of the Peter Principle. The Peter Principle states that people are continually promoted until they eventually reach their level of incompetence. The best way to deal with this boss is to do whatever you can to help.

Mean bosses. Fortunately, these bosses tend to self-destruct over time. Therefore, they are not frequently encountered. How does one deal with such bosses? Usually it is a futile effort to try to reason or argue with this type. The best tactic is to steer clear of these bosses as much as possible.

Competent but lazy bosses. These bosses are capable and able to do the job but lack proper motivation. At best, they do just enough to get by. This behavior makes it especially hard for the bosses' subordinates to perform well. The best approach with these bosses is to do your job in such a manner that they are forced to work. Possible actions include regularly asking these bosses for input, taking problems to them, and scheduling regular conferences to review general progress.

Laissez-faire bosses. Laissez-faire bosses are worse than the lazy ones because these types don't care. As with mean bosses, laissez-faire bosses usually self-destruct. Thus, the best tactic is to bide your time and do the best you can under the circumstances. Examples of laissez-faire bosses include those close to retirement, those who have been passed over for promotion, and those who are planning to take another job.

SOCIALIZING WITH OTHER MEMBERS OF THE ORGANIZATION

Should supervisors socialize with their employees? Should supervisors socialize with their superiors? These are questions that sooner or later confront almost every supervisor. Take for instance the person who is promoted to supervisor over his or her former peers. The situation is especially complicated if this person frequently socialized with other members of the old work group (as a member of the bowling team, a poker group, etc.). There are no hard and fast answers to these questions. However, some general guidelines that should be followed are:

1. Don't be overly anxious to socialize with subordinates or superiors—let things take a normal course of events.
2. Use common sense—don't do anything stupid while socializing that will later cause problems (such as getting highly intoxicated at a party at the boss's house).
3. Be yourself—don't try to put on a false front to impress your boss or other superiors.
4. Don't try to use your rank when socializing with subordinates.
5. Don't make any work-related promises to subordinates while socializing.

Chapter 20

MANAGING SUPERVISORY TIME

Most supervisors could improve their efforts if they would use their time more effectively. A common complaint of supervisors is that if just a little more time were available, they could catch up. However, nobody gives us time and we cannot buy it; we already have all the time we are going to get. Better achievement depends on only one thing—making better use of the time available. It is not a question of how many hours were worked but of how those hours were spent.

All supervisors have more or less the same amount of time. Successful supervisors know how to use their time wisely. They do not permit their time to be used up on meaningless tasks.

TIME USAGE

To start using the available time more effectively, it is helpful to find out how it is being spent at present. What tasks are being performed, and how much time is being spent on each? Tally sheets can be used to record the activity or nonactivity occupying each 30-minute work period. By recording such data for a few weeks, a matrix of time and activities results. Characteristic work patterns can be deduced from these data, as can the time spent for each major work classification, expressed as a percentage of total time. For example, it may be found that 20 percent of a supervisor's time is spent on paperwork and 11 percent on instructional and developmental efforts each month.

Using these data as a base, pertinent questions can help interpret what the data mean. Are these activities appropriate for the supervisor to undertake? Is adequate time being given supervisory planning and counseling? Are any important supervisory duties being short circuited?

145

Should any present activities be reduced or eliminated? Answers to such questions can lead to a better pattern of time expenditures.

Sorting necessary activities into categories enhances the effectiveness of time management. The following categories are commonly used: (1) routine, (2) normal, (3) special, and (4) innovative. Routine activities should not require the time of the supervisor. They are best delegated to others who know how they should be performed. Normal activities are bona fide supervisory work that occurs as a consequence of fulfilling the job of supervision. They account for the great majority of a supervisor's time. Special activities are similiar to normal activities, with the exception that they are usually of a nonrecurring type. Innovative activities represent efforts to develop and use new ideas in supervising the work performance effort. While relatively small in amount, innovative time is essential and should be allowed for if the supervisor is to progress. The importance of setting aside time and earmarking it for creativity cannot be overemphasized. It is a mistake to ignore the importance of having time to think about and develop improvements.

Activities can also be sorted into other categories. Some supervisors obtain good results by dividing their time into time spent on (1) daily operations, (2) preventing problems, and (3) creative thinking. The proportion devoted to each category depends upon the supervisor's specific job, but most time will be given to the first group, daily operations. This pattern of time distribution points out that not all of the supervisor's time is spent on immediate operations such as direct work efforts, outlining procedures to group members, or interpreting company policy. Some time will be given to the prevention or correction of problems and to creative efforts to discover or explore opportunities.

Special assignments can pose supervisory problems. They are difficult to plan for because they occur irregularly, may require considerable time, and usually are unlike previous tasks performed. Few supervisors have not at some time or another been asked to write a special report, serve on a project, or try out some new idea of work performance or machine operation.

Although it is difficult to time budget special assignments and subject them to time management, the effort should be made to do so. It is helpful not to schedule regular activities too tightly so that some time may be taken from them for special assignments without serious difficulty. An alternative is to make the needed adjustments by simply reducing some of the allotted times and applying them to special work.

This disrupts the original plan, but all schedules are tentative and should be considered flexible to some degree.

TIME PLANNING

Each act performed by supervisors should move them closer to their supervisory objectives. To do so, long- and short-term goals must be defined, priorities established, and activities concentrated at any given time on specific undertakings. By following effective time planning, the supervisor can determine whether the work is progressing on schedule.

Time planning promotes "time consciousness" on the part of the supervisor. As already noted, because time is irreplaceable it should never be wasted. Activities such as merely passing the time of day with colleagues, needlessly repeating instructions, and holding useless meetings should be minimized or even eliminated when possible.

The use of a weekly planning sheet similar to that shown in Figure 20–1 is recommended. This is a spread sheet that gives a total picture of the week's planned efforts. A check mark designates the period

FIGURE 20–1
Weekly planning sheet for supervisors

Activities	Mon. A.M.	Mon. P.M.	Tues. A.M.	Tues. P.M.	Wed. A.M.	Wed. P.M.	Thurs. A.M.	Thurs. P.M.	Fri. A.M.	Fri. P.M.
Dept. meeting	✓									
Industrial Inst.		✓	✓			✓				
Weekly repor										✓
Safety meeting						✓				
Routine	✓		✓		✓		✓		✓	
Develop new methods						✓		✓		✓

Weekly Plan Sheet

Week ending _____   Name of supervisor _____

planned for each task. As activities are completed, a circle is drawn around the check mark. A glance at the sheet shows what is planned for the day, and how the time has been spent.

Some supervisors realize improvements in time use by cutting down gradually on those tasks which require the most time. If the schedule shows two hours are to be taken for the task of preparing a report, the time allotted should be reduced to one and one-half hours and an attempt made to see if the same task can be accomplished within this shorter period. If not, one and three-quarters hours can be tried. Much saving of time can be derived from small segments—a little bit here, a little bit there. Normally, large timesaving segments—several hours or a half day—are not available.

ESTABLISHING GOOD WORK HABITS

When one stops to consider the letters, reports, memos, telephone calls, meetings, visitors, and reading material that the average supervisor is faced with each day, it is not hard to see where an entire day can be spent on communication alone. Although communication is an important part of the supervisor's job, there are many ways of managing the time spent in the communication process.

Paperwork. A supervisor who is not swamped with paperwork is rare. Most supervisors must keep some employee records, prepare or assist in preparing various reports, write letters and memos, and stay current by reading newsletters, magazines, and trade journals.

One suggestion for dealing with paperwork is to categorize it as you go through it. Basically, there are three classes of paperwork. These are:

1. Requires action by the supervisor.
2. Needs reading, passing on to someone else, or filing.
3. Needs to be thrown away.

Class three can be identified and thrown away immediately. Class one and class two must be handled more carefully, but there are also effective means of dealing with these classes. One suggestion is never to set aside a piece of correspondence until you have done something with it or decided what needs to be done about it.

Letters and memos. Letters and memos are one of the more common types of communication that fall into class one. Action should be taken on most letters without putting the letter down. Handwritten responses on the bottom of the letter are usually acceptable. Use form letters for responses whenever possible.

If you have a secretary, you should consider the use of a dictating machine. Giving dictation directly to your secretary wastes time because two people are tied up at the same time on the same letter or memo. Furthermore, many letters and memos can be answered directly by your secretary. However, you should be sure that your secretary has enough information to answer the letter or memo. Delegating the authority to answer certain letters and memos increases a secretary's job scope and can be a source of motivation to the secretary. Finally, the phone can often be used in lieu of a letter.

Report writing. Many of the suggestions for handling letters and memos also apply to report writing. Plan the report completely before you start writing. Use a dictating machine whenever possible. Keep the report as short as possible while covering the material that needs to be covered. Also, write the report for the reader. Big words and long sentences may impress the reader but may not get across the message.

Filing. Most people have a filing cabinet full of material that they will never look at again. Knowing what to save and what to throw away is not easy. When deciding whether something should be filed or not, answer the following questions:

1. Is this on my "useful filing" list?
2. How can I get this information if I ever needed it, and it isn't in my files?
3. How (exactly) am I going to use this piece of paper within the next 12 months?[1]

After answering these questions, a supervisor can better decide whether or not to file something. One additional suggestion is to go through and clean out your files at least once a year. Throw away material that you haven't used during the year.

Reading material. Most people have a stack of reading material that they intend to read "one of these days." Unfortunately, one of these days never comes and the stack just gets higher and higher. One way to lessen this problem is to improve your reading skills. If your organizations offers a seminar on reading skills, ask to attend it.

---

[1] Donna Niksch Douglas and Merrill E. Douglas, "Timely Techniques for Paperwork Mania," *The Personnel Administrator*, September 1979, p. 21.

Also, many colleges and universities offer reading skills improvement courses.

Another suggestion for handling reading materials is to skim the table of contents or the major headings. If either one of these looks interesting, you might read the entire material. Otherwise, you should probably throw it away.

Meetings. One of the biggest time-wasters is meetings, which eat up more time than most supervisors want to admit. Some meetings are undoubtedly not necessary. These should be eliminated. Necessary meetings should be carefully planned. Chapter 6, Communicating with Employees, offered some specific suggestions for holding effective meetings.

Telephone. The telephone can either save or waste a lot of time. Too many supervisors allow the telephone to run their day. If you have a secretary, you should have the secretary hold your calls when you are in an important meeting. When you are on the phone for business reasons, you should realize that the time of two people is being tied up. Be polite, but make your point and get off the phone. Nothing is wrong with telling a caller in a polite manner that you have to get off the phone.

Visitors. Supervisors often have many expected and unexpected visitors. Salespeople are a common example. Visitors can take up a lot of unnecessary time. One time-saver in this area is to establish a policy of not seeing visitors who have not made an appointment. If someone does get to you and you don't want to visit with that person, don't sit down. Talk standing up. This communicates that you don't expect the meeting to last long. On scheduled visits, let the visitor know how much time you have scheduled for the meeting and stick to this time.

ADDITIONAL SUGGESTIONS FOR TIME MANAGEMENT

Proper delegation (see Chapter 5) is a major key in a supervisor's effective use of time. As was mentioned earlier, a most serious time-waster is a supervisor doing work that should be handled by a subordinate. Delegation frees a supervisor to do the more important tasks of supervision. Delegation also teaches subordinates to think for themselves, to make decisions, and to produce effective results.

Supervisors should avoid spreading their efforts so thinly that they are ineffective. Supervisors should also concentrate on what they are doing at any given time and not jump from project to project. Jumping from project to project generally means that not one of them gets done properly. Valuable time is wasted in starting one project, dropping it to start another, and then coming back to the first project at a later time.

Deadlines should be used. Deadlines provide wanted and needed targets and assist in getting the work accomplished. Many tasks carry their own deadlines—work orders, reports, and so forth, but others do not. On these, supervisors should put a date for completion. This helps supervisors to better schedule their time and to accomplish all projects on a timely basis.

Chapter 21

DEVELOPING YOURSELF

To grow mentally is a must for a supervisor. Mental growth helps a supervisor to keep pace with the present job requirements, to qualify for promotion, and to enjoy life. Success in supervision depends a great deal on a person's efforts to improve. However, these efforts should be directed toward specific goals, be carefully defined, and be related to the present and future opportunities. Furthermore, self-improvement is a self-perpetuating force. Once a program is started, it usually becomes a permanent part of a person's thinking and behaving.

SELF-DEVELOPMENT PROGRAMS

A self-development program can be overly broad. It is best to concentrate on relatively few actions at any given time, master them, and then move forward to the next logical step. To keep a self-improvement program on target, it is suggested that a written schedule be prepared and that actual accomplishments be periodically compared to the sched-

FIGURE 21–1
Format for scheduling self-improvement program

Improvements sought	Year One	Year Two	Year Three	Comments
Cut grievances	Take course in labor relations			Start community college night class in September
Safety	Hold monthly meetings			Hold meetings first Tuesday of each month 8–8:30 A.M.
Activity in organizations	Join supervisor's club			Get active in this group
Computer knowledge	Read two books			Get suggested titles from library

ule. Figure 21–1 presents a format that might be used. Periodically ask yourself (1) if areas selected for improvement remain valid, (2) if progress in making the improvements is satisfactory, and (3) if you are experiencing greater self-confidence.

EDUCATION

Increasing knowledge through education is one of the best and most widely used means for self-development. A person must have a positive attitude toward education and put forth the required effort to gain the most from educational efforts. Forget the idea that you are too old for schooling and studying. It is never too late to start improving yourself through education.

Education offers a wide variety of choices. Organizational training programs are popular, and many of them are excellent. University courses offer breadth of subject content and new views. Many colleges offer evening courses for the convenience of working students. Correspondence courses can be done at home and provide a variety of general as well as specialized courses.

Seminars conducted by professional associations and universities stress discussions and the exchange of ideas. In addition, they offer the opportunity to talk informally with other supervisors. Reading selected books helps update your knowledge and enlarges your comprehension in your field. Consult your organization or public library for suggested readings. Likewise, periodicals on supervision are excellent for up-to-the-minute developments concerning what other organizations are doing in the supervisory area. In addition, memberships in professional associations are helpful. Their programs and activities can be quite beneficial. A number of national, regional, and local associations exist. To select a good group, talk with your friends or consult with your personnel department.

OTHER APPROACHES FOR SELF-DEVELOPMENT

Another common approach used in self-development is to ask for suggestions from your boss, other supervisors, and the personnel managers of your organization. These people are generally most willing to help those who want to improve themselves and who are determined to do so. You can also observe how other managers handle crises, assign work, motivate people, and reach decisions. Frequently, you cannot duplicate their ways because of the differences in situations, but you can acquire some helpful knowledge.

Keeping a notebook always handy and jotting down information worth remembering is another aid to personal development. Most people forget things unless they make a written note. In time, you can build a permanent record of many useful ideas.

Volunteering for special assignments, committees, service groups, and the like can give you experience and the opportunity to assist. These activities also put you in the spotlight and give you favorable publicity. Thus, promotion possibilities are enhanced at the same time you are developing yourself.

Set high-performance standards for your personal supervisory efforts. Don't be satisfied with average accomplishments. Try to be outstanding—reach and strive for the best.

Adopt a somewhat aggressive attitude. Push for improvements and for new ideas. Evaluate your current status objectively and seek ways to improve it. Display enthusiasm in your work, but be sincere about it. Avoid the defensive strategy of explaining why such and such can't be done. Such a viewpoint hampers self-improvement.

Don't give up easily. Many problems are solved and a promotion won by hanging in there. Self-development is a slow process. It often takes longer to reach a given level of self-improvement than you thought it would.

Finally, keep in mind that as a supervisor you are hired basically for your talent and time. Your job is not simply to fill a job. Make certain that what you have to offer is being utilized. This depends in great measure on how you select and apply your self-development efforts. Others can advise, but you must furnish the attitude, initiative, and application to make your self-development a reality.

"THINK TIME"

Thinking is a natural human activity. It is an excellent method of self-help. The secret of doing something well is to spend some time thinking about it. Supervisors should reserve a fixed place and time for thinking. The first or last 15 minutes of each workday are generally good "think times." This helps to ensure that time to think has priority. To begin your thinking, skim the areas or things you deal with. Give preference to those areas which you feel have some potential for improvement. Make no attempt to find the solution or improvement at this stage. It may come later—either spontaneously or after concentration. During these initial stages, you should merely try to identify the areas. Next, select an area that needs improvement. Concentrate on this single area. Look into various elements of this area without being concerned whether a possible thought for its solution is feasible or not. Jot down your thoughts and ideas. If you find a solution is not forthcoming, proceed to the next identified area and repeat the process for this new area. You will find that ideas for one area help in coming up with solutions in another area. Out of all of this will emerge tentative answers. They may result from logical handling of your thoughts and ideas but more likely will emerge when you least expect them—early in the morning when you arise, late at night while listening to music, or while watching a sporting event.

Employing think time is helpful in becoming mentally sharp and more alert. In times of difficulty, people commonly turn their thoughts to other, brighter things. Thinking helps to ease the difficulty, to find a way out, and to achieve solutions to problems that otherwise would not be possible.

CREATIVITY

Closely associated with self-improvement and think time is creativity. Creativity governs progress. The best solution to a supervisory problem may not be found by logical deduction of known facts, but by thinking up a new idea that uses an entirely new concept. Creativity can likewise play a major role in the development and advancement of a supervisor. Everyone can be creative. It is not a mysterious power given to a select few. Typically, the person who believes "creativity is not my bag" has never tried to use his or her creative powers. One key to being creative is to concentrate. Think of only one problem or subject at a time and strive to get as many different ideas as you can. Forget about whether they are practical or not. The initial step is to get a volume of ideas. The evaluation of each idea takes place later. Also important is the use of your unconscious brain. To do this, rest your conscious mind when you feel tired. The unconscious brain takes over and reviews and relates thoughts the conscious mind produced. Commonly this is called "sleeping over the problem." In addition, be persistent. Keep trying because useful ideas seldom result from the first attempts. You may well go over many ideas before you discover the one suited for the situation. Last, implement the idea. This can be a difficult step. It has been said that the most difficult task in the world is to drive an idea through the skull of a human being. As was discussed in Chapter 17, the common reaction to a new idea is to turn it down. "It's not practical," "We have tried that before," and "Too much time will be required" are typical reactions.

Figure 21–2 presents some suggestions for gaining acceptance of your ideas.

FIGURE 21–2
How to get your ideas accepted

1. State the problem and why it needs to be solved. If a current practice is to be revised, explain why the change is necessary or desirable.
2. Prepare a rebuttal for each of the several possible turndowns you feel might be given.
3. Stress the benefits of your idea. Support your viewpoint with factual data such as a short payback period, lower direct labor cost, and safer working conditions.
4. Make your presentation complete by including answers to each objection likely to arise in implementing your idea. In essence, this means less, not more, work for the person to whom the idea is being presented.

Examination 1—Chapters 1-7

_____ 1. The supervisor's work is heavily oriented toward motivating and controlling. (T or F)

_____ 2. Technical knowledge, but not human relations and administrative skills, is required to be a successful supervisor. (T or F)

_____ 3. Supervisors usually have more subordinates answering directly to them than any member in the higher level of management. (T or F)

_____ 4. The supervisor of today hires, fires, sets the conditions of work, and is virtually unchallenged in what is decided. (T or F)

_____ 5. Most supervisors are promoted from the ranks of operative employees. (T or F)

_____ 6. The use of authority alone will normally enlist support and cooperation of subordinates. (T or F)

_____ 7. Being decisive means making the decision in the least time possible. (T or F)

_____ 8. A successful supervisor will not make a decision until _all_ of the facts are known. (T or F)

_____ 9. Which should be used when speed is of greatest concern: _a._ group decision making, _b._ individual decision making?

_____ 10. Brainstorming is a form of group decision making that involves presenting a problem and then allowing the group to develop ideas for solutions. (T or F)

_____ 11. A successful supervisor treats all decisions with equal importance. (T or F)

_____ 12. A supervisor's success depends upon understanding the targets that are to be achieved with a given period. (T or F)

_____ 13. It is important to relate work goals to the employee's goals whenever possible. (T or F)

_____ 14. The successful supervisor will generally attempt to express objectives in nonquantifiable terms. (T or F)

_____ 15. The objective setting process should involve those responsible for achieving the objective. (T or F)

_____ 16. The supervisor's power to reward or punish is emphasized in the management by objectives style. (T or F)

_____ 17. Objectives should remain constant, rather than be changed and updated. (T or F)

_____ 18. Allocating and scheduling work means the same thing for all practical purposes. (T or F)

_____ 19. Planning is primarily concerned with future decisions. (T or F)

_____ 20. Controlling is basically a passive checkup; no work is accomplished per se by controlling. (T or F)

_____ 21. The supervisor's planning is typically.
   a. Short range.   c. Intermedi ate range.
   b. Long range.   d. None of these.

_____ 22. Controlling usually takes place after the planning has been completed and implemented. (T or F)

_____ 23. A Gantt chart
   a. Defines the sequence and manner in which the various components of a product are assembled.
   b. Outlines what happens to a product as it progresses through a department.
   c. Helps to visualize and simplify the scheduling problem.
   d. Is a meteorological test for predicting the weather.

_____ 24. Competent supervisors make all the major decisions in their departments. (T or F)

_____ 25. The nature of authority and responsibility determines the proper role of a supervisor. (T or F)

_____ 26. Successful supervisors normally learn to utilize the informal organization. (T or F)

_____ 27. Delegation of responsibility means abdication of responsibility by the delegating part. (T or F)

_____ 28. A supervisor's authority is determined by upper levels of management and is implemented through the organization structure. (T or F)

_____ 29. Staff authority is used to support and advise line authority. (T or F)

_____ 30. Communication is so vital to the supervisor that it is virtually impossible to communicate too much. (T or F)

_____ 31. In communication, the conveyance of facts and all the facts will secure the receiver's conviction. (T or F)

_____ 32. For communication purposes, the informal organization is usually
  a. Highly effective.   c. Poorly accepted.
  b. Extremely accurate.   d. Generally ignored.

_____ 33. For communication to be effective it must be
  a. One way.   d. A positive way.
  b. Two way.   e. A negative way.
  c. Three way.   f. None of these.

_____ 34. Loyal supervisors ignore the grapevine but answer all questions put to them completely and honestly. (T or F)

_____ 35. The key to motivation is getting employees to want to do a job. (T or F)

_____ 36. The real contribution coming from McGregor's work with Theory X and Theory Y is the understanding that a leader's attitude toward human nature has a large influence on how the person behaves as a leader. (T or F)

_____ 37. A common motivator today is
  a. An understanding   d. Job enrichment.
     supervisor.   e. All of these.
  b. Pay.   f. None of these.
  c. Employee
     intelligence.

_____ 38. Job enrichment involves giving a worker more of a similar type of operation to perform. (T or F)

_____ 39. The thrust of Maslow's theory is that a satisfied need is not a motivator. (T or F)

_____ 40. According to Herzberg, those factors which motivate people are factors related to the work itself as opposed to the work environment. (T or F)

Now check your answers with the correct ones on page 168.

Examination 2—Chapters 8–14

_____ 1. All learning is self-learning. (T or F)
_____ 2. In developmental work, the supervisor should remember that the best sequence is from
    _a._ The very difficult to the very easy, so the trainee is advancing to increasingly less difficult material.
    _b._ The very easy to the very difficult, so that the progression is to increasingly difficult material.
    _c._ A mixture of very difficult and very easy, so that the trainee maintains a practical and balanced view of the material.
    _d._ The beginning to the end of the work, so that the trainee fully realizes the practical work makeup.
_____ 3. The primary need for employee development is to make employees able to contribute more effectively to the accomplishment of stated goals. (T or F)
_____ 4. A supervisory training program should be designed for supervisors and not by them. (T or F)
_____ 5. The orientation program begins during the hiring process for a new employee. (T or F)
_____ 6. Orientation programs are overdone in most organizations. (T or F)
_____ 7. A group has become a team when
    _a._ Free exchange of ideas takes place, and members support and assist one another.

b. It is rare for one member to kid another.

c. There is little resistance to outsiders.

d. Superiors declare the group to be a team.

_____ 8. For group dynamics to be most effective, unanimity of purpose is essential. (T or F)

_____ 9. The supervisory approach followed normally depends upon

a. The situation.

b. The group included.

c. The supervisor's nature.

d. All of these.

e. None of these.

_____ 10. In general, when group members reach a certain size, the group has become a team. (T or F)

_____ 11. A group norm is an understanding among the group members about how the members of the group should behave. (T or F)

_____ 12. The chances are usually best for achieving a strong team effort when there are several work activities to be performed. (T or F)

_____ 13. Most employees do not like to appraised. (T or F)

_____ 14. An effective way to improve performance appraisal is for the supervisor to

a. Concentrate on those traits or incidents that are of prime importance.

b. Give emphasis to the employee's work during the most recent four weeks, since it is best remembered.

c. Include consideration for the employee's potential, not simply what the person has or has not accomplished.

d. All of these.

e. None of these.

_____ 15. A key consideration in counseling by a supervisor is

a. Do not ask any questions, let employees do all the talking.

b. Practice sympathy—always show sympathy for employees.

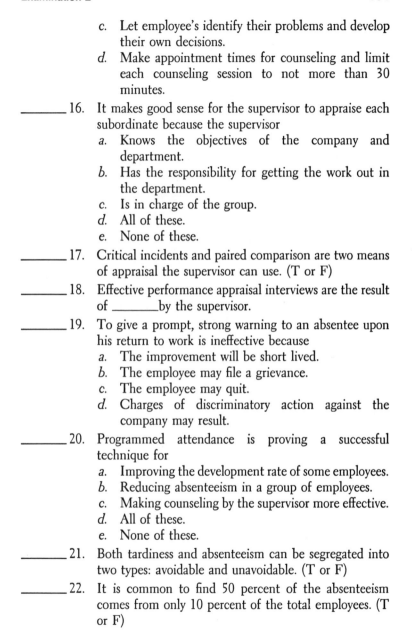

    c. Let employee's identify their problems and develop their own decisions.

    d. Make appointment times for counseling and limit each counseling session to not more than 30 minutes.

_____ 16. It makes good sense for the supervisor to appraise each subordinate because the supervisor

    a. Knows the objectives of the company and department.

    b. Has the responsibility for getting the work out in the department.

    c. Is in charge of the group.

    d. All of these.

    e. None of these.

_____ 17. Critical incidents and paired comparison are two means of appraisal the supervisor can use. (T or F)

_____ 18. Effective performance appraisal interviews are the result of _____ by the supervisor.

_____ 19. To give a prompt, strong warning to an absentee upon his return to work is ineffective because

    a. The improvement will be short lived.

    b. The employee may file a grievance.

    c. The employee may quit.

    d. Charges of discriminatory action against the company may result.

_____ 20. Programmed attendance is proving a successful technique for

    a. Improving the development rate of some employees.

    b. Reducing absenteeism in a group of employees.

    c. Making counseling by the supervisor more effective.

    d. All of these.

    e. None of these.

_____ 21. Both tardiness and absenteeism can be segregated into two types: avoidable and unavoidable. (T or F)

_____ 22. It is common to find 50 percent of the absenteeism comes from only 10 percent of the total employees. (T or F)

_____ 23. Employees with fewer years of employment tend to be on time more than older employees. (T or F)

_____ 24. A favorable supervisor-subordinate relationship helps to keep tardiness at a low level. (T or F)

_____ 25. Conflict is something that should always be avoided. (T or F)

_____ 26. Intrapersonal conflict means conflict that is internal to the individual. (T or F)

_____ 27. Causes of interpersonal conflict include
   a. Opposing personalities.
   b. Prejudices based on personal background.
   c. Jealousy and envy.
   d. All of these.
   e. None of these.
   f. A and c only.

_____ 28. Structural conflict is independent from the personalities invovled. (T or F)

_____ 29. Intrapersonal, interpersonal, and structural conflict many times are planned by the people involved. (T or F)

_____ 30. Supervisors most frequently deal with interpersonal and intrapersonal conflict.

_____ 31. Most minority group members
   a. Require different supervisory practices from majority group members.
   b. Fulfill various types of jobs successfully.
   c. Constitute a potential threat to the performance of the supervisor's duties.
   d. Are limited in their capacity for development.
   e. All of these.
   f. None of these.

_____ 32. Of all the women workers in the United States, most work to supplement their family income. (T or F)

_____ 33. Few older employees gain much satisfaction from their work. (T or F)

_____ 34. Affirmative action programs promote preferential treatment of persons who are members of minority groups. (T or F)

_____ 35. Quotas for hiring minorities are required by law. (T or F)

_____ 36. Employees with special problems that interfere with their behavior and performance may be suffering from serious illnesses or emotional disturbances. (T or F)

_____ 37. A problem employee is an employee whose job performance is affected by personal problems that cannot be corrected with normal counseling or disciplinary measures. (T or F)

_____ 38. A large number of organizations are beginning to institute employee assistance programs based in large part on cost savings. (T or F)

_____ 39. Once a problem employee has been identified, the supervisor must confront the employee. (T or F)

_____ 40. The supervisor does not bear the primary responsibility for evaluating rehabilitation. (T or F)

Now check your answers with the correct ones on page 169.

Examination 3—Chapters 15–21

_____ 1. Some grievances filed represent imagined feelings of injustice employees have about employment relationships. (T or F)

_____ 2. An important prerequisite for the supervisor in attaining good labor relations is
   a. Knowledge and support of the company's philosophy and policies.
   b. Insistence upon getting all the facts regarding every grievance presented.
   c. Complete knowledge of the contents of the current contract.
   d. Prompt attention to every grievance presented.
   e. All of the above.
   f. _B_ and _d_ only.

_____ 3. An effective means for handling a grievance procedure is for the supervisor to refer it to the personnel department, where it can be settled. (T or F)

_____ 4. The union steward is to the union what the supervisor is to the company. (T or F)

_____ 5. Formal grievance procedures are applicable only to unionized organizations.

_____ 6. In a unionized organization, the supervisor has a dual responsibility. (T or F)

_____ 7. A formal discipline procedure usually begins with a written warning, followed by an oral follow-up warning. (T or F)

_____ 8. Discipline should be aimed at correction and punishment. (T or F)

_____ 9. In order to maintain effective discipline, the supervisor _____follow the rules that the employees are expected to follow.

    a. Must always.

    b. Should usually.

    c. May or may not.

    d. Doesn't have to.

_____ 10. Supervisory decisions to discipline after a period of lax enforcement contribute to poor morale and reduced productivity. (T or F)

_____ 11. When a decision to discipline an employee is questioned, a supervisor bears the burden of proof. (T or F)

_____ 12. The hot stove rule emphasizes that discipline should be directed against the act rather than against the person. (T or F)

_____ 13. Match the type cost (left column) with the appropriate description (right column):

a. Indirect labor costs.	1. Expenditures for physical space, research, and legal services.
b. Supplies costs.	2. Expenditures for machine operators, assemblers, and packers.
c. Overhead costs.	3. Expenditures for cost clerk, elevator operator, and methods analysis.
d. Direct labor costs.	4. Expenditures for necessary items that do not become part of the service or product.

_____ 14. Overtime is a common example of overhead costs. (T or F)

_____ 15. The supervisor is a key person in cost-reduction efforts. (T or F)

_____ 16. For maximum effectiveness, cost reduction should be concentrated at any one time in one department of an enterprise.

_____ 17. Match the term (left column) with the description (right column):

a.	Progressive budget revision.	1.	A useful and detailed plan providing an overall pattern of cost information for a stated period.
b.	Periodic budget revision.	2.	Revisions are made every two months for the following six-month period.
c.	Moving budget revision.	3.	Major adjustments are made three times a year.
d.	Budget.	4.	Revisions are made monthly for the following 12-month period.

_____ 18. Incentives should not normally be offered as a reward for cost reduction. (T or F)

_____ 19. The use of a safety committee is highly desirable because it sees to it that the safety program is enforced. (T or F)

_____ 20. Most employees don't believe that accidents can happen to them. (T or F)

_____ 21. Unsafe personal acts cause the bulk of organizational accidents. (T or F)

_____ 22. An accident frequency rate indicates the frequency with which disabling injuries occur. (T or F)

_____ 23. Many organizations and supervisors are antagonistic toward OSHA because they feel threatened by OSHA inspections. (T or F)

_____ 24. It is the supervisor's responsibility to ensure that all safety rules are followed by the employees. (T or F)

_____ 25. Supervisors should have fixed moral standards and abide by them. (T or F)

_____ 26. Even if the supervisor is perceived as being slightly unethical or dishonest, most employees are not likely to feel that similar behavior on their part is acceptable. (T or F)

_____ 27. Organizational politics refers to the practice of using means other than good performance for bettering your position in the organization. (T or F)

_____ 28. Almost any approach to organizational politics can be ethical or unethical depending on how it is used. (T or F)

_____ 29. In dealing with dishonest subordinates, the supervisor must gather proof of the subordinates' dishonesty by documenting the word of others. (T or F)

_____ 30. The best approach in dealing with mean bosses is to steer clear of them as much as possible. (T or F)

_____ 31. It is a fact that some supervisors have more time than other supervisors do. (T or F)

_____ 32. A simple way to improve time is to gradually reduce those tasks that require the most time. (T or F)

_____ 33. Because of their impersonal nature, form letters should not be used when responding to a letter or inquiry.

_____ 34. Time planning promotes time consciousness on the part of the supervisor. (T or F)

_____ 35. Normally, a supervisor should not waste time on "creativity," that is, thinking about and developing improvements. (T or F)

_____ 36. Research has shown that most people lose the ability to pick up new ideas easily around the age of 55.

_____ 37. Supervisors should reserve a specific place and time for thinking. (T or F)

_____ 38. The initial step in developing creativity is to get a volume of ideas. (T or F)

_____ 39. A self-development program cannot be overly broad. (T or F)

_____ 40. To be creative, a supervisor should use his unconscious brain to review and relate thoughts the conscious mind has produced. (T or F)

Now check your answers with the correct ones on page 171.

Answers to examinations

EXAMINATION 1—CHAPTERS 1–7

1. T Normally a supervisor spends a good deal of time on motivating and controlling.
2. F Human relations and administrative skills are also required. (See Figure 1–3.)
3. T Their interaction also tends to be face to face with employees.
4. F Many staff specialities help today's supervisor.
5. T Those with good technical skills and good work records are usually promoted.
6. F It can be just as important to know when not to use authority as when to use it.
7. F Being decisive means making a decision in a reasonable amount of time.
8. F It is rare that a supervisor ever knows *all* the facts.
9. a Individual. Group decisions almost always take longer.
10. T No criticisms of solutions are allowed initially.
11. F Some decisions are more important than others.
12. T A supervisor must understand his or her objectives.
13. T This can motivate employees.
14. F Wherever possible, objectives should be quantified.
15. T Most employees want to participate.
16. F The emphasis is on goal attainment.
17. F Objectives should be updated as necessary.
18. F Resource allocation determines what work will be performed by what person and/or machine; scheduling develops the precise timetable to be followed.
19. F Planning is concerned with the future impact of today's decisions.
20. F Good control efforts can be encouraging and helpful to employees.
21. A It is the nature of supervisor work to deal with day-to-day operations.

22. T   Control means knowing what is happening in comparison to what was planned.
23. C   A Gantt chart does not necessarily deal with a product.
24. F   Competent supervisors delegate.
25. T   What decisions are made and what obligations exist are determining factors.
26. T   The supervisor can use it to disseminate information and to consult with informal leaders.
27. F   The delegating supervisor is still ultimately responsible.
28. T   The organization structure establishes the lines of authority.
29. T   Staff authority is normally limited to making recommendations to the line personnel.
30. F   Some things are best not said; too much communication can confuse.
31. F   The receiver's interpretation of facts is also important.
32. A   The grapevine is the communication system of the informal organization.
33. B   Information should flow back and forth between the sender and receiver.
34. F   Smart supervisors use the grapevine as a supplement to formal communication.
35. T   Motivation must come from within the employee.
36. T   A leader's attitude does influence the types of behavior exemplified by the employees.
37. D   The job itself is the important factor.
38. F   Job enrichment involves upgrading the job by adding motivator factors.
39. T   According to Maslow, once a need is satisfied the individual is then motivated by the next higher level need.
40. T   Proper attention to the "hygiene" factors will keep an individual from being dissatisfied but will not motivate the individual.

EXAMINATION 2—CHAPTERS 8–14

1. T   Whether or not learning takes place is determined by the trainee.
2. B
3. T   This enables the employee to make the maximum contribution.
4. F   To be fully effective, a supervisory training program should be designed by supervisors.

5. F The orientation program begins after the employee is hired.
6. F The reverse is true; often orientation programs do not exist.
7. A
8. T
9. D Depends on all three.
10. F When group members support and assist one another on their own, the group has become a team.
11. T
12. F Chances are best when there is a single work activity.
13. F Most employees want to be appraised.
14. E Not one of these statements is in keeping with prescribed appraising practices.
15. C
16. D However, some believe appraisals by several raters are preferable.
17. T Others are rating scales, rankings, forced choice, and MBO.
18.   Good planning.
19. A Such action has only temporary effect; it is addressed to the symptom, not the cause.
20. B Under this approach the supervisor and group agree to an acceptable absentee rate.
21. T
22. T Furthermore, about 50 percent of the work force will have perfect attendance.
23. F To the older person, the job is very important.
24. T
25. F Conflict can have positive effects; the key is to manage it properly.
26. T Interpersonal conflict is among people.
27. D All of these can lead to interpersonal conflict.
28. T Structural conflict results from the nature of the organizational structure.
29. F Only strategic conflicts are often planned and intentionally started.
30. T Structural and stragetic conflict are more prevalent at higher levels.
31. B
32. T
33. F Work is likely to be the center of their interest and efforts.
34. F It is generally agreed that employers that are required to have affirmative action programs must make special efforts to increase the number

of minorities in the work force but *without* discrimating against others.

35. F Quotas are not required by law; however, written goals may be required under affirmative action guidelines.
36. T
37. T Remember, all employees have some personal problems.
38. T Employee assistance programs can result in considerable savings.
39. T Most supervisors do not relish this responsibility.
40. F Evaluating the success of rehabilitation must be based on job performance, and the supervisor is in the best position to make this evaluation.

EXAMINATION 3—CHAPTERS 15–21

1. T Whether imagined or real, a grievance exists if the employee believes it does.
2. E
3. F Usually the supervisor should handle a grievance.
4. T The steward is the employee's advocate.
5. F Nonunionized organizations can have formal grievance procedures.
6. T The supervisor fulfills the contractual obligations of management and sees that the union fulfills its obligations.
7. F The first step is usually an unrecorded oral warning.
8. F Discipline should be aimed at correction rather than punishment.
9. A The supervisor sets the example!
10. T A supervisor should use discipline consistently.
11. T A supervisor should always follow accepted guidelines when disciplining.
12. T Personalities should not be a factor when applying discipline.
13. A–3; B–4; C–1; D–2.
14. F It is direct labor cost.
15. T The supervisor is in an ideal position to do something about costs.
16. F Cost reduction should cover all areas.
17. A–2; B–3; C–4; D–1.
18. F If employees believe that cost reduction is in their best interests, they are more likely to participate.
19. F The safety committee's normal duties do not include enforcement.

20. T They can happen to the other person, but not to me!
21. T Unsafe personal acts have been estimated to cause 80 percent of all organizational accidents.
22. T
23. T Few laws have evoked as much reaction as OSHA.
24. T This is an integral part of a supervisor's job.
25. T Remember, the supervisor sets the example.
26. F A supervisor's general attitude toward ethics can greatly affect employee ethics.
27. T Self-interest is usually the motivating force.
28. T
29. F Proof of dishonesty must be based on evidence and not the word of others.
30. T These bosses will destroy themselves over time.
31. F All supervisors have the same amount of time; the important consideration is how they use it.
32. T Small savings here and there are important.
33. F The use of form letters can save considerable time!
34. T Time awareness promotes time efficiency.
35. F This is an excellent method of self-help.
36. F We are aware of no such findings! It is never too late to learn.
37. T The first or last 15 minutes of each workday are generally good think times.
38. T These ideas can be evaluated later.
39. F It is best to concentrate on relatively few actions at any given time.
40. T This is commonly called sleeping over the problem.

Glossary/Index

173